The Practical Plutarch

by

Anne E. White

CONTENTS

Prologue

In 2007, Anthony Esolen wrote a list of the "Top Twenty Books That Nobody Reads." First on the list was Plutarch's *Lives of the Noble Greeks and Romans*.

At the time, I was surprised that it was even included—I mean, to make it to the list of famous books that nobody reads, it would have to be famous, if not read, right? Everybody's heard of *The Grapes of Wrath* and *The Odyssey* and *Paradise Lost*, even if they don't read them. But it seems to me that more people haven't heard of Plutarch's *Lives* than have heard of it but don't read it.

Part of the reason, I think, is that Plutarch is kind of hard to find unless you're looking on purpose. You're not going to see multiple copies of Plutarch's *Lives* come up at book sales like you are the hundreds of school editions of Shakespeare's plays. If you're talking to homeschoolers who are even aware of Plutarch's existence, they're most likely either of a classical or a Charlotte Mason bent, since Charlotte enthused about the *Lives* in her own books and they were a fixture in the PNEU curriculum. Even the writer Penelope Lively, who received her early education through the Parents' Union correspondence school, says (in her memoir *Oleander Jacaranda*) that she can't understand what a child would have gotten out of Plutarch.

Also, Plutarch was a "moral biographer," and that's apparently gone out of style. But that's good for us, in some ways, because you don't have to know all the history to make sense of one of Plutarch's *Lives*. Some background does help, but it isn't really the battles and the names of kings that matter; it's what makes a great leader, or a poor one; what good choices were made, and what bad ones.

And then there's the problem of whose translation you're looking for, and which *Lives* are included in the volume you have. And the problem of some of the nasty stuff—Plutarch is neither squeamish nor prudish. Lacking an edited version, you have to read him aloud rather than turning students loose to forage as they will.

However, for the past two decades, the Charlotte Mason educational community has quietly been turning all this ignorance of Plutarch's *Lives* on its ear. All AmblesideOnline students over the age of ten are encouraged to study one of his *Lives* every term—beginning with retellings if they want, but eventually moving on to the grownup version. Since there seemed to be no handy guide out there, we began to create our own notes. And over the years, we've heard from families for whom Plutarch is no longer a stranger; and from teachers who say that the *Lives* are inspiring enjoyable classroom discussions, and even (sometimes) loud arguments.

This, from a book at the top of the list of the Books That Nobody Reads. Not bad.

Notes: "Welcome to the Party" is adapted from a talk given at l'HaRMaS in 2016. Some other bits of the book began as blog posts, but they have been disassembled and reconnected as needed.

Since in a previous book I referred to Charlotte Mason as "Charlotte" (vs. Mason or Miss Mason), it made sense to continue the same style here. Charlotte Mason/PNEU vocabulary is explained in the Glossary.

And finally...you may notice that some of the thoughts here come from a specifically Christian worldview. I do not apologize for that, but I do think it's fair to mention it. Those with other beliefs may find similar references within their own faith traditions.

Part I: Welcome to the Party

"If we want to offer ideas by the means of early history in the form of biography, we come at once to Plutarch, the prince of biographers. We take the children straight to the fountain-head and introduce them to this dear deliberate old gentleman, who will, in a leisurely way, tell them delightfully graphic stories in simple language and who will not omit a single detail, so that even the child can think of no more questions to ask."

(Miss Ambler in *The Parents' Review*)

In Which Plutarch Plays Host

At the annual l'HaRMaS gathering in Kingsville, Ontario, the speakers are referred to as "cultivators," since each one tends his or her own "patch of ground." (A *harmas* is a piece of wild, seemingly useless ground). One year, when I was asked to talk about my bit of cultivating for the past few months, I decided to share the work I had been doing on Plutarch.

I wondered what Plutarch himself would have written, if he had decided to write the *Life of Plutarch*? He might have said that he was a Delphic priest; that he served as the mayor of his home town, Chaeronea, in Greece; and that he was also the local police commissioner. In an essay called "Advice on Public Life," he forewarned visitors that they might find him busy supervising building construction in Chaeronea. He seems to have been a sort of Roman-Empire Benjamin Franklin, only without the inventions.

Charlotte Mason's students know Plutarch best for the biographies of famous Greeks and Romans that make up his *Parallel Lives*; but those make up less than half of his surviving works. The rest, called the *Moralia*, are made up of all kinds of other things which Plutarch happened to find interesting: essays on literature, religious issues, the education of children, technical philosophical essays, something called *Should an Old Man Take Part in Public Life?*, advice on how to listen to lectures, how to tell a flatterer from a friend, how to avoid offensive self-praise, and advice to a bride and groom. He also wrote a collection of dialogues, called the *Symposiacs* or *Table Talk*, based on actual dinner parties that he hosted as part of his public duties in Chaeronea.

Christopher Pelling, the author of a recent edition of Plutarch's *Life of Julius Caesar* (which is where I found the list of essay topics), wrote,

> "Plutarch's dinner guests might be members of his family, might be local farmers or doctors, or might be visiting members of the Roman elite. These men of power can exchange intellectual conversation, even if their contributions are usually not the most learned and scholarly of all; they know how to behave on such occasions..."

Plutarch spent time tending his own "patch of ground"; and he found it just as stimulating to hear what other people had been doing and

3

thinking about. He enjoyed good company and good talk. He knew how to have some "fun that was funny."

"Fun that is funny" is a phrase from Dr. Seuss, and it was used more recently in Jan Karon's Mitford novel *Somewhere Safe With Somebody Good*. Coot Hendrick, a middle-aged man who has had a hard, somewhat restricted life, and who is just now learning to read, reads *The Cat in the Hat* to his hundred-year-old mother as she is dying. Throughout the rest of the story, he looks for ways to have "fun that is funny," as he begins to connect in new ways with the people around him. In our culture, we tend to miss out on the idea that our minds and our spirits need fun too, or refreshment and renewal if you prefer; but the Greeks, including Plutarch, understood its importance. Education is a discipline, but it is also an atmosphere and a life.

Andrew Kern of the Circe Institute wrote that when we experience "delightful leisure, we can open our eyes to honour and virtue, engage in a pleasant humanizing conversation with some truly wise people, and repent of our miserable miserliness." Which is, more or less, what Coot Hendrick was finally able to do...to join the party and discover "delightful leisure," or "fun that is funny."

Honoured Guests (not Shadows)

But how do we get through the door to Plutarch's dinner party? And what do we do once we're there?

One way is to sidle quietly in as a Shadow. In an essay written many years ago about Plutarch, Ralph Waldo Emerson said that "the guests not invited to a private board by the entertainer, but introduced by a guest as his companions, the Greeks called shadows." Plutarch himself said that he wouldn't go to a party as a shadow guest; it wasn't a classy thing to do, and if you've ever been in a situation like that, it's awkward. However, we are not required to take on that role here; we have in our hands what Laurie Bestvater calls the "Grand Invitation."

Still, entering a room full of strangers can make the most gregarious of us hesitate. When we jump into reading Plutarch's *Lives* for the first time, we can feel like we're in an unfamiliar place, with unfamiliar people, speaking an unfamiliar language. How do we go from feeling like strangers at Plutarch's party to friends, and how do we welcome others in? This book is intended to ease the nerves of newcomers; and perhaps it will have something for the veterans as well.

Poke Around

The first thing we need to do at this party is to find out who's there, who these people are. Plutarch is sometimes vague (to us) about things that were familiar to his audience, because the events were a background to what he was more interested in: the people themselves, the choices that they made, and the whole question of leadership and citizenship. In the Bible, you can read the story of David and Goliath without needing much information on the Philistines; but when you get to the Babylonian captivity and suddenly there's a Persian king instead, you need some extra explanation. It's like reading a mystery novel set on a ship, and the ship happens to be called the *Titanic*. For us, that's self-explanatory, but two hundred years from now, it might require a footnote.

So the sheer amount of unfamiliar references in one of Plutarch's *Lives* can be overwhelming, like trying to meet everyone at a conference and remember all their names and where they're from. The easiest way in real life is to start with the person sitting beside you: you talk to them, and then maybe they'll introduce you to an old friend or to someone else they've just met. The same thing applies to Plutarch; and in that sense it's convenient that each of his *Lives* is a distinct package, even though each one is also full of other overlapping lives and sometimes he also includes ancestors or poets or other people not actually involved in that story. One of our challenges as readers of Plutarch is not to get too sidetracked by those rabbit trails; but the longer we stay at the party, the more sense each story makes. We start to notice if a particular Greek lived before, during, or after the Golden Age of Athens, or if maybe he was from Sparta or from the boonies out in Epirus; if he was around during the Peloponnesian Wars; or if he was affected (like Eumenes) by the rule of Alexander the Great and the political upheaval that followed his death. The *context* of a person's life matters, and even knowing the place they come from isn't always enough; the time is important too. Agis and Cleomenes were two kings of Sparta, but they lived in an era when the glorious ideal of being a Spartan warrior had become a kind of joke, and they wanted to get things back on track. One of the threads in Roman history is about the struggle for power between the Senate and the common people, and their fear of kings and dictators. Julius Caesar (both his life and his death) didn't happen in a vacuum; there was a lot of background behind him, and the more you know, the more you can make sense of what he did and the way that the people around him reacted.

Pay Attention

The second thing is, listen to the conversation. Pay attention to what people are saying, how they're saying it, who they're talking to, and how those other people are responding. In Plutarch, we have to read what's there, and sometimes more than once, because Plutarch uses long sentences and doesn't always explain who his pronouns are referring to; and then we have the additional problem of needing to read him in an English translation, and that might be one that uses unfamiliar grammar and vocabulary. Thomas North translated Plutarch's *Lives* from French to English in the sixteenth century (even before the King James Bible was completed); and John Dryden translated them from Greek to English a hundred years later. Dryden is said to be more scholarly, but he can also be stiffer, dryer to read. Charlotte recommended North's translation; but *Parents' Review* articles mentioning Plutarch include quotes from later translations such as the one by John and William Langhorne, so they didn't seem to have anything against reading alternative versions (see Appendix D).

I personally enjoy reading North's, and it's what I mostly use for the AmblesideOnline study notes (although the Eumenes study in this book uses Dryden's); but I do not think we are violating a PNEU principle if we try out a different translation. If difficulty in language means the difference between reading Plutarch in a contemporary translation and not reading him at all, I would say to read the newer one; you might be missing some of the "riches" of language and thought, but it is better than giving up entirely.

Sidebar: Why I Like North's Translation

The same passage, translated three ways:

> But the Carthaginians who were left in Rhegium

perceiving, when the assembly was dissolved, that
Timoleon had given them the go-by, were not a little
vexed to see themselves out-witted, much to the
amusement of the Rhegians, who could not but
smile to find Phoenicians complain of being
cheated. (Dryden)

But the Carthaginians in Rhegium, after Timoleon
had put to sea and the assembly had been dissolved,
were indignant, and in their discomfiture afforded
amusement to the Rhegians, seeing that, though
Phoenicians, they were not pleased with what was
effected by deceit. (Bernadotte Perrin, *Loeb
Classical Library* edition)

But the captains of the Carthaginians, that were in
Rhegium, when they knew that Timoleon was under
sail and gone, after that the assembly of the Council
was broken up, they were ready to eat their fingers
for spite to see themselves thus finely mocked and
deceived. (Thomas North)

Good Company

So we can't afford to doze off at Plutarch's dinner party; but staying awake is worth it. Here is a story we might hear while we're listening.

In 367 B.C., Dion was the uncle of the young king Dionysius of Syracuse, which was a Greek colony in Sicily. Dionysius had grown up under a brutal, suspicious father who had not allowed him any education or training in character (he was only allowed to make little wooden toys); and now that he was king himself, he was pretty clueless. Dion had enough power in Syracuse that he could have gotten Dionysius deposed and set up a people's government; but he thought it would be better to try to improve Dionysius's worldview before going to that extreme. So he called up his friend Plato and invited him to come over from Athens and give some lectures.

What happened next in Syracuse was sort of a Plato-mania. Plutarch said, "There was a general passion for reasoning and philosophy, insomuch that the very palace, it is reported, was filled

7

with dust by the concourse of the students in mathematics who were working their problems there." The trouble was that Dionysius was suddenly becoming so smart, so much improved by all this mathematics and philosophy, that it made the powerful men in Syracuse nervous, because they liked having a stupid king who wouldn't cause them any trouble. Rumours started flying. People said that Dionysius might be going to "to dismiss a navy of four hundred galleys, disband an army of ten thousand horse and many times over that number of foot, and go seek in the schools an unknown and imaginary bliss, and learn by the mathematics how to be happy." Maybe it was all a plot by Dion to take power in Syracuse.

So what happened? The dinner guest telling the story decides to tease us, saying we'll have to find out the rest for ourselves. But he gives us a hint: "build mistrust." Plant seeds of doubt, make people question their friendships and loyalties, even destroy each other.

Suddenly we realize that we totally get what this story's about, even if we don't recognize all the cultural details or remember the names of all the characters. It's a plot as old as the Bible and the *Iliad*, and as new as the latest spy or romance novel. We think about what we would do if we were Dionysius, or Dion, or one of the young people doing math in the palace dust. It's not such a dull party after all, because we've been listening. Plutarch's *Lives* started out for us as a bit of seemingly wild, useless ground; but we see it is teeming with life when we get down on our knees and take the time to look closely. And the coolest part is that we have been listening to the same story, in the same way, as Charlotte Mason read it, Montaigne and Rousseau read it (in French), Emerson read it, Shakespeare read it, Abraham Lincoln read it, and Frankenstein's monster read it (in German). If we ever run into some of these people in another life, we can talk about Dion and Syracuse, and Publicola, and the Gracchi brothers. Maybe we'll even get to talk *to* Publicola and the Gracchi brothers.

Potluck

The third thing we need to do is bring our own contribution to the party; and that doesn't mean dessert. Ask questions back, agree or disagree, think about alternatives. And it doesn't matter if the insights come from adults or children; we can all share equally.

Welcome to the Party

Christopher Pelling said that Plutarch's visitors might not be "the most learned and scholarly of all," but they knew what made a good party. That means we are welcome too.

But just in case you need some extra inspiration and company, I found a poem by Ralph Waldo Emerson, "Written at Rome," and these are the first few lines:

ALONE in Rome. Why, Rome is lonely too;—

Besides, you need not be alone; the soul

Shall have society of its own rank.

Be great, be true, and all the Scipios,

The Catos, the wise patriots of Rome,

Shall flock to you and tarry by your side,

And comfort you with their high company.

Virtue alone is sweet society,

It keeps the key to all heroic hearts,

And opens you a welcome in them all.

Ten Interesting Things You Can Learn from Plutarch's *Lives*

1. Lycurgus's idea for forcing the Spartans to shop local: get rid of gold and silver, and make only heavy, ugly coins from iron that every other state would make fun of and refuse to accept. Simple.

2. Solon's insistence that every couple deserved a honeymoon: "The bride and bridegroom shall be shut into a chamber, and eat a quince together."

3. Solon's law against dogs that bite: "He made a law, also, concerning hurts and injuries from beasts, in which he commands the master of any dog that bit a man to deliver him up with a log about his neck, four and a half feet long; a happy device for men's security."

4. Why swimming lessons can pay off if you're taken hostage but have better things to do: "...the young girls went down to the river to bathe...and, seeing no guard, nor any one coming or going over, they were encouraged to swim over...Cloelia, passing over on horseback, persuaded the rest to swim after; but, upon their safe arrival, presenting themselves to Poplicola, he neither praised nor approved their return, but was concerned lest he should appear less faithful than Porsenna...but he looked on her with a cheerful and benignant countenance, and commanding one of his horses to be brought, sumptuously adorned, made her a present of it." (*Life of Poplicola/Publicola*)

5. Creative uses for parsley: "As he was mounting a hill, beyond which he expected to see the camp and army of the enemy, there met him some mules loaded with parsley...[they say that] when a man is dangerously ill, that he is ready for his parsley. Wishing to rid them from this superstition and to stop their fears, Timoleon halted them, and made a suitable speech, pointing out that their crown of victory had come of its own

accord into their hands before the battle, for this is the herb with which the Corinthians crown the victors at the Isthmian games, accounting it sacred and peculiar to their own country…So Timoleon, having addressed his soldiers, as has been said, first crowned himself with the parsley, and then his officers and men did so likewise." (*Life of Timoleon*)

6. How to be un-insultable: "The enemies of Fabius thought they had sufficiently humiliated and subdued him by raising Minucius to be his equal in authority; but they mistook the temper of the man, who looked upon their folly as not his loss, but like Diogenes, who, being told that some persons derided him, made answer, 'But I am not derided,' meaning that only those were really insulted on whom such insults made an impression; so Fabius, with great tranquility and unconcern, submitted to what happened, and contributed a proof to the argument of the philosophers that a just and good man is not capable of being dishonoured." (*Life of Fabius*)

7. Why you should be careful what you pray for: "[Camillus] lifted up his hands to heaven, and broke out into this prayer…'if, in the vicissitude of things, there may be any calamity due, to counterbalance this great felicity, I beg that it may be diverted from the city and army of the Romans, and fall, with as little hurt as may be, upon my own head.' Having said these words…he stumbled and fell…" (*Life of Camillus*)

8. How to catch an enemy with laundry: "But one of the sumpter-horses, which carried the furniture for his tent, having fallen that day into the river, his servants spread out the tapestry, which was wet, and hung it up to dry; in the meantime the Pisidians made towards them with their swords drawn, and, not discerning exactly by the moon what it was that was stretched out, thought it to be the tent of Themistocles, and that they should find him resting himself within it; but when they came near, and lifted up the hangings, those who watched there fell upon them and took them." [*Life of Themistocles*]

11

9. Why spray paint should have been invented sooner: "As Themistocles sailed along the coasts, he took notice of the harbours and fit places for the enemy's ships to come to land at, and engraved large letters in such stones as he found there by chance…in which inscriptions he called upon the Ionians to forsake the Medes, if it were possible, and to come over to the Greeks…"

10. The funniest line in the *Life of Themistocles*, but one that's been attributed to others as well: "Laughing at his own son, who got his mother, and by his mother's means, his father also, to indulge him, he told him that he had the most power of any one in Greece: 'For the Athenians command the rest of Greece, I command the Athenians, your mother commands me, and you command your mother.'"

Part II: Dusting off the Treasure

"The nearer the history comes to our own time, the fuller it becomes of political and constitutional details, and the more we are involved in questions of statecraft. If, however, we go back to the early history, we find it moves on broader, simpler lines, and the statesmanship, so far as it exists at all, only shows how a resourceful mind attempts to cope with circumstances."

(Miss Ambler in *The Parents' Review*)

Return to the Castle

You know the part of *Prince Caspian* where the Pevensie children come back to Narnia, not realizing that many years have gone by in Narnia-time? They accidentally find their ruined castle, and then they go down into the vault and find the weapons and the other gifts that once belonged to them. C.S. Lewis's description of the piles of treasure is a picture of immeasurable wealth and abundance. But he also says that "the treasures were so covered with dust that unless they had realised where they were and remembered most of the things, they would hardly have known they were treasures."

What is the treasure that, though hidden and dusty, is there waiting for us to claim it and own it? "The best thought the world possesses," wrote Charlotte Mason, "is stored in books" (*Philosophy of Education*, p. 26). We can trust in the books themselves, and in children's natural desire for knowledge, which makes the whole thing suddenly much simpler, if we can focus on the substance of the books, and not so much the mechanics of teaching. We need to use them in a way that makes use of all the intelligence and imagination that are already in our children, and the habits and skills, the powers of attention and observation and persistence, that they are learning.

Some people find it strange that the PNEU programmes defined so strictly what was to be done, since Charlotte emphasized the value of the mind and the person. Setting definite goals for the term's work encouraged continual progress, but at a reasonable pace. Daily timetables were also suggested, for a variety of reasons which included *not* keeping children at their desks too long. Each student had a certain number of memory assignments—though those could vary, they were specific things like "Two hymns by Keble." Each one was expected to keep a nature journal and, when old enough, history records and other notebooks. Each one was expected to complete certain handicrafts and projects, such as sewing a child's dress. Each one was to be learning arithmetic, French, etc.

But what wasn't spelled out in the programmes is more "suggestive," as Mason might say: what the children were supposed to think about such and such a fairy tale, what ideas they were supposed to take from a passage of Plutarch, or what vocabulary they were to have learned from a science chapter. The freedom given within a

PNEU term was not in the assignments ("find three catkins and three tree buds"), but in the ideas; in each student's digestion of all this material, each one's response, and each one's growth. This is why "we narrate and then we know," to quote one *Parents' Review* article. When we use Mason's methods, we allow children the same treatment we want for ourselves: allowing them the freedom of poking around, helping them develop the skill of paying attention, and encouraging their additions to the potluck (or, more formally, the Conversation).

Some people think of education as connecting the pieces of a jigsaw puzzle. This agrees with the viewpoint of the boy mentioned in *Philosophy of Education* who was delighted to discover that "everything seems to fit into something else." However, we should prefer an image not of putting in the thousandth piece and being "done," but of continuing to build up our picture—extending it outside the original frame if necessary—to acquire an ongoing education, fired by our human longing to reconnect scattered pieces.

> "A personal, soulful home takes time, and ideally
> draws equally from these three components: the
> glory days of the past, a possibly busy and bland
> present, and whatever the bright-eyed future holds.
> It will be painfully slow to put together—that's OK."
> Paige Rien, *Love the House You're In*

Claiming Ownership

Marva Collins was a teacher in Chicago who became well known for her unorthodox (yet very classical) approach to teaching inner-city students. In her first book, she wrote about taking her class to a screening of the film *The Man Who Would Be King* (based on a story by Rudyard Kipling), with a lecture afterwards on his life. When her motley crew entered the theater, the lecturer himself approached them and objected, saying there had been "some mistake." She insisted that they be allowed to enter. Most of the students in the audience were older and seemed interested mainly in getting an afternoon out of class; but Collins' students asked good questions, and one of them corrected the lecturer on a fact about Kipling's life. Collins wrote that, while she didn't want to encourage "pedantry," she allowed them to have their say, proving that her students had engaged themselves with the subject as well as, or better than, the more "privileged" students, and that they were, in fact, an unusually appreciative and delightful audience.

There can be both an arrogance and a hesitance about reading a book which used to be common currency but which is now reserved for academics. Neither of those attitudes is necessary. We need the courage, and we need to encourage others, to enter the treasure vaults and lecture halls that we have been told are off-limits. One of Marva Collins' frequent themes can also help us here: that we can claim any story, essay, poem, play, as our own, no matter who we are or when we live. This idea has been explored in novels such as *The Guernsey Literary and Potato Peel Pie Society*, where a group of readers are each handed a different book that helps them survive the terrible events of wartime occupation. One character later writes a letter, saying,

> "Some of [the books the others were reading]
> sounded all right, but I stayed true to Seneca. I
> came to feel that he was talking to me—in his funny,
> biting way—but talking only to me...Everyone is sick
> of Seneca, and they are begging me to read someone
> else. But I won't do it."

Another example is *Brave New World*, set in a dystopian time when books are kept locked away for the powerful few, but where one character's self-education with only a volume of Shakespeare's plays provides him with the power of independent thought. This "claiming" also happens quite literally at the end of the 1966 film version of *Fahrenheit 451*, where each character "becomes" a book by memorizing its contents. Can we ourselves become Plutarch's *Lives*? Perhaps if we encounter them one by one, for a term or a season, we will be able to see something of our own "Brave New World" in ancient Greece and Rome, and to find something of ourselves in each *Life*; to join the party, but then to come home again. The Seneca-reading character ends his letter with these words:

> "I am glad the war is over, and I am John Booker
> again."

To Spend the One and to Meet the Other

Here's a Plutarch story that comes from Rome, from the century before Julius Caesar. It's about two brothers named Tiberius and Gaius, who grew up in a privileged home, but who became aware of big injustices in the Republic. One thing they saw was a huge amount of unemployment and overcrowding in the poorer parts of the city. Where were all these people coming from? It turned out that a lot of them were from the rural areas of Italy. They had lost their family holdings because of wars that had ruined their land, and because their husbands and sons had been lost to those wars, and because wealthy people were buying up the farms and turning them into the Roman equivalent of factory farms. Many of them hoped that they could get jobs or start businesses in the city, but that didn't always happen.

Tiberius was the older brother by several years, so he was the first to get into politics and try to fix the system, by getting elected as a tribune, which was a sort of watchdog position in the government, looking out for the rights of the people. As soon as he got into office, he started working on ways of redistributing the land more fairly. That made some powerful people angry at him, partly because he was overstepping the limits of being a tribune. He managed to get himself killed in a riot, while his supporters were arrested and put to death, including one man who was reportedly put in a barrel with poisonous snakes.

What the people in power hadn't counted on was that Tiberius was so admired and popular, that he had other supporters and friends, and people saw him as a martyr and a hero, so they allowed some of his work to continue, as a way to keep the peace. Still, after a few years it seemed like the Roman social justice thing was old news: until Gaius Gracchus decided it was time for him to pick up his brother's vision.

So now I have a job for you to do, and you can have some "fun that is funny." Coming up is a passage from Plutarch's *Life of the Gracchi*. I have shortened and edited it a little. I have also broken it into dialogue, perhaps something you might hear in a conversation at Plutarch's dinner party. I would like you to do four things with the passage. The first is to read it through. The second is to mark or circle a few of the words or phrases that you think would be the most important to pre-discuss with the students with whom you would most likely to be reading Plutarch. You don't have to write the meanings, just mark anything that catches your eye as going to cause a problem. Try to keep it to about half a dozen words. The third thing is to write one question or discussion point that this passage brings to your mind. In other words, add yourself into the conversation. (There's a bit of space left below for notes.)

Plutarch: So tell me, what happened to Gaius Gracchus after his brother was murdered?

Tall Guest: At first, either for fear of his brother's enemies, or designing to render them more odious to the people, he absented himself from the public assemblies, and lived quietly in his own house, as if he were not only reduced for the present to live unambitiously, but was disposed in general to pass his life in inaction.

Sleepy Guest: What's wrong with that? Too much ambition can get you in trouble.

Short Guest: And some indeed, went so far as to say that he disliked his brother's measures, and had wholly abandoned the defense of them.

Tall Guest: However, he was not but very young, being not so old as Tiberius by nine years; and he was not yet thirty when he was slain.

Short Guest: In some little time, however, he quietly let his temper appear, which was one of an utter antipathy to a lazy retirement...he was not the least likely to be contented with a life of eating, drinking, and money-getting.

Hungry Guest: What's wrong with that? Pass the grapes.

Short Guest: He gave great pains to the study of eloquence, as wings upon which he might aspire to public business; and it was very apparent that he did not intend to pass his days in obscurity.

Tall Guest: It is the prevailing opinion that Gaius was a far more thorough demagogue, and more ambitious than ever Tiberius had been, of popular applause.

Fun Guest: What's wrong with that? Let's start the karaoke contest.

Short Guest: Yet it is certain that he was borne rather by a sort of necessity than by any purpose of his own into public business.

Tall Guest: There's that weird story your uncle Cicero told about Gaius's brother sending him a message.

Plutarch: His brother who had died? How is that possible?

Short Guest: The story goes that when Gaius would have lived privately, his brother appeared to him in a dream, and calling him by his name, said, "Why do you tarry, Gaius? There is no escape; one life and one death is appointed for us both, to spend the one and to meet the other in the service of the people."

Finding the Sweet Spot

We have very little specific instruction on how the teaching of Plutarch's *Lives* was to be accomplished.

The PNEU programmes gave only a bare outline of what was to be accomplished in a term's readings. Blackie's edited texts offer a short glossary at the back of the book (only twenty words for the entire *Life of Julius Caesar*!); and students were encouraged to use extra reference materials (see Appendix D); but, overall, it seems that not much was done to provide context, or to suggest ways of retaining the material beyond an oral or written narration. We may draw on what we know about PNEU lessons from history, Bible, and other subjects, but there are one or two added difficulties here. First is the language, although for students who are learning to read Shakespeare, the King James Bible, and other older books, this is not insurmountable. A bigger hindrance, however, is the fact that the history and Bible lessons build on each other not only from lesson to lesson but from term to term; Plutarch's *Lives*, however, are not (and should not be) taught chronologically. Every term brings a reset of time and place, and an often brand-new list of people, cities, kingdoms. As we go on, more and more of them do become familiar; but it's often difficult to remember the difference between Antigonus Monopthalmus and Antigonus Gonatus, between Aristides and Alcibiades. Even I often have to go back and remind myself who was who and when was when. In most of the Roman lives, it's necessary to know something about their government, what a consul and a tribune and a censor were, and how being consul also made you a general of the army if there was a war. If nobody has ever explained that it was normal for the Spartans to have two kings at once, how would you be able to follow the story of Agis and Cleomenes?

And that brings us to the million-drachma question: do those background things matter? And how much do they matter? Let's be very careful about assuming that young students will find interest in the same details that we do as teachers, especially if they have only read two or three of the *Lives*, but we ourselves have covered many of them, many times, and are starting to notice new connections which we're eager to share. I have an image, here, of a Sunday School classroom that I knew years ago, furnished with maps of everything from the

Israelites' journey to Paul's travels; and I remember, with an embarrassing flash of honesty, how completely uninteresting they were to me. Yes, he went to Antioch. Yes, it's on the map. Next?

What did Charlotte herself have to say about the how-to's?

> [Students] may read some fifteen of these Lives,
> which I think stand alone in literature as teaching
> that a man is part of the State, that his business is to
> be of service to the State, but that the value of his
> service depends upon his personal character. The
> Lives are read to the children almost without
> comment, but with necessary omissions. Proper
> names are written on the blackboard; and, at the
> end, children narrate the substance of the
> lesson. (*School Education*, p. 280)

And what did her teachers have to say about it?

> "We do not tell the tales, we know we cannot, we
> read them as well as we know how and without
> comment, unless questions are asked. We rely upon
> the imagination of the children to work upon this
> material until it becomes theirs, and I think we do
> not deceive ourselves by so doing." (E.A. Parish
> in *The Parents' Review*)

Please note Miss Parish's small comment there about "unless questions are asked." If the students are interested enough to be confused, they will ask questions, and the teachers had better know at least where to look for the answers. And you can't always depend on what your book says about it (see Appendix B).

Another teacher, known only as "Miss Ambler," wrote one of the only *Parents' Review* articles we have which is specifically about teaching Plutarch. After quoting some lines from one of the *Lives*, she says,

> Could there be a better opening for a few words on
> obedience? The words, however, must only be very
> few, and used more to direct the working out of the
> train of thought in the child's mind, and must
> therefore depend upon the child and the point of
> view he takes. Again, a few pages further on in the
> same "Life," we have the idea of self-control, self-

victory. And, here again, there is no ostentatious
pointing of a moral... In order to insure the
complete assimilation of the ideas, it would perhaps
be helpful if homely but quite impersonal examples
of their application to every-day life were given.
(Miss Ambler)

So the "words must be few" and must "depend on the child," which
makes it a bit difficult if we are teaching a group. However, even Miss
Ambler hints that there might be more to helping students visualize a
Plutarch story than a straight reading without any description.

All these ideas might be driven home by making use
of the dramatic situations which Plutarch never fails
to seize, and by gathering up the principal points to
make a vivid word-picture.

Allowing students to create a mental word-picture is the heart-and-soul
of many of Charlotte's lessons, from picture study to spelling to
narrating *Ivanhoe*; and it may give us a key to teaching Plutarch as well.
Many of us will remember reading the notes about an early-years Bible
lesson, in which Charlotte recommends J. Paterson Smyth's
commentary for children. I am going to include the whole passage
here, because I think it could be quite helpful.

Between the ages of six and twelve children cover
the whole of the Old Testament story, the Prophets,
major and minor, being introduced as they come
into connection with the Kings. *The teacher opens
the lesson* by reading the passage from *The Bible for
the Young*, in which the subject is pictorially
treated; for example,—

*"It is the battle field of the valley of Elah. The camp
of Israel is on one slope, the big tents of the
Philistines on the other. The Israelites are rather
small men, lithe and clever, the Philistines are big
men, big, stupid, thick-headed giants, the same as
when Samson used to fool them and laugh at them
long ago. There is great excitement on both sides,"*
etc.

There will be probably some talk and discussion

after this reading. *Then* the teacher will read the
Bible passage in question which the children will
narrate, the commentary serving merely as a
background for their thoughts. The narration is
usually exceedingly interesting; the children do not
miss a point and often add picturesque touches of
their own. *Before the close of the lesson*, the teacher
brings out such new thoughts of God or new points
of behaviour as the reading has afforded,
emphasising the moral or religious lesson to be
learnt rather by a reverent and sympathetic manner
than by any attempt at personal application.
(*Philosophy of Education*, pp. 162-163, italics mine)

Before I apply this to Plutarch, I have to make one point, especially for
those of us who read this passage years ago and then tried to apply it
as gospel (if you'll excuse the expression) in teaching Bible lessons.
Bear with me, it does apply to the way we teach Plutarch as well. In the
above passage, the "visualizing" part comes first, and the Bible lesson
isn't given until the end of the lesson. I have read variations on this,
such as a *Parents' Review* article which says, "The reading is followed by
narration, and *then* by such teaching [as is given in the *Bible for the
Young*]." And that seems to agree more with the instructions given in
the term programmes for younger students:

Teacher to prepare beforehand; in teaching, read
the Bible passages ONCE and get the children to
narrate; add such comments (see Paterson Smyth)
as will bring the passages home to the children.

So either Charlotte had forgotten things in her old age; or someone
else wrote that section of the book for her, and misfired; or there was
more than one acceptable way of approaching such a lesson. I tend to
go with the last one. If a lesson plan supports Mason's educational
principles, and it helps students to learn enough of the material to care
about the ideas, then it's all good.

So, assuming that there is probably more than one "right" way to
approach a Plutarch term or lesson (including some families' custom
of reading very short daily amounts), what are our "best practices,"
with or without study guides? Here are a few suggestions:

1. Plan to spend at least part of the first lesson on context, even if that means shortening the reading a bit, or adding in a special first-week introduction (as Charlotte's teachers sometimes did with their "oral lessons"). Review whatever students already know that could apply to this study. Maybe they have read about an earlier time when someone was young, and in this story that person is still around but he's old. Maybe there were some beautiful buildings going up in an earlier story, but now they are neglected and falling apart. In the story of *Agis and Cleomenes*, the kings want to recover their neglected Spartan culture; and the students may already know quite a lot about that. Or, for example, in *Dion*, the story takes place in a Greek colony in Sicily; many students will think of Sicily as part of Italy, so it will make sense to them that the Greeks living there felt somewhat cut off from the politics and culture of their homeland. Use whatever means you can to open the door.

2. "Proper names are written on the blackboard…" Every name, place, and other proper noun used in a lesson? That can be a lot of names, and sometimes grandfathers and fathers and sons repeat names. Like seeing the cast of characters at the beginning of an unfamiliar play, the names are somewhat meaningless until you have something to connect with them; and the more of them there are, the more confusing it gets. And, oh dear, there are often variations of spelling and translation as well. (Is it Caius or Gaius? Spain or Hispania?) I would suggest sticking to a few major and/or unfamiliar names, and being a little bit flexible with students' attempts at spelling them. This is also a place where certain types of creative/alternative narrations may help: for instance, the character cards suggested for *Eumenes*.

3. "…we read them as well as we know how and without comment, unless questions are asked." This is sometimes hard! We are assuming here that the teacher is reading aloud to the students, unless you are in a situation (perhaps with older students) where they can share in the reading, or where they would prefer to read silently to themselves. If you are the one

who reads aloud, do your best to make it effective! Try to look up the pronunciation of names you don't know (my intuition about Greek names is almost always wrong). Go slowly and read with expression. Have you ever noticed how a good reader on an audio book can bring it to life, even without trying to do fancy character voices? On the other hand, have you ever heard somebody read one of your favourite Bible passages in a mumbling monotone, and wanted to throw something at them? Lack of attention to the reading can kill even a good story; and since these *Lives* are often difficult and unfamiliar, we need to be super-attentive to our delivery. For younger students, you might try asking them ahead of time to listen for a certain repeated name or word, and react in a certain way, such as putting up their hands, adding something to a drawing, or moving counters from one place to another every time they hear it. This isn't something to do every time, but just something else to have in the toolbox.

4. "The narration is usually exceedingly interesting; the children do not miss a point and often add picturesque touches of their own." That, again, depends on each reading not being too long (you can narrate after each paragraph, or even after each sentence if you are just starting out). It assumes that there is access to unfamiliar names; and that other rules of narration are followed, such as no interruptions. And the same principles apply to written narrations.

5. "Before the close of the [Bible] lesson, the teacher brings out such new thoughts of God or new points of behaviour as the reading has afforded…" "…it would perhaps be helpful if homely but quite impersonal examples of their application to every-day life were given." This is where we get into a tough place, between the shibboleth that "[Plutarch] leaves the conscience and judgment of his readers to make that classification," and not wanting to say "this is a lesson about honesty" when a student is more interested in some other point. We don't want to point fingers and say "that's just like when you failed your last test because you didn't study"; but we do

want to emphasize (somehow) that the story shows people's character traits and how they demonstrate them; what choices they make, and how those choices affect others.

There is a continuum between saying too little (or absolutely nothing), and saying too much. Some of us are more comfortable at one end of it than the other. All of us will, probably, cross the line occasionally, but we are human after all. If you find yourself on the talk-too-much side, try pulling back a bit; ask one question like "What would you have done?" and let the conversation go from there. If, on the other hand, you cannot think of any way to say "Look how courageous he was there!" without it feeling artificial, then try asking the same question. If you are using the *Plutarch Project* guides, choose one of the suggested discussion questions for that lesson, and see where the students want to take it.

6. "All these ideas might be driven home by making use of the dramatic situations which Plutarch never fails to seize, and by gathering up the principal points to make a vivid word-picture." After the students narrate and ask any questions they have, the teacher does a little narration as well, not as correction but more as corollary. An example for *The Gracchi*: "Can you imagine what it must have felt like for Licinia to see her husband going out the door? She might have felt angry and sad, but she knew that he wanted to do what was right for Rome. Do you think it was as difficult for Gaius? I remember when my own brother went to overseas to teach; it was very hard to see him leave and not know when we would see him again. I trusted God to take care of him, but I still missed him. It takes a lot of courage to do something that makes us feel afraid." That's just an imaginary example, and I'm sure you can come up with better (real) ones.

On *Hogan's Heroes* and Plutarch

Recently we have been watching a few episodes of *Hogan's Heroes*, and it occurred to me that one reason the show is still fairly watchable is that certain aspects of its humour are timeless. I don't mean just from the supposed 1940's, when the show is set, to the 1960's, when it was made, and now to this century, but across the ages. If a Roman soldier had been given that DVD and something to play it on, he would, I am sure, have recognized a particular weak-chinned commander-in-charge, who, though a tyrant over his own men and the prisoners of war that they guarded, was so afraid of being demoted or, worse, "sent to the Russian front" (insert Roman equivalent) that he became the world's best boot-kisser whenever his superiors were around. The soldier would have been familiar with a middle-aged, not-too-clever sergeant who had been dragged out of his comfortable home life to participate in yet another war; he would perhaps have recognized some of the prisoners' bribes and tricks to get information or other favours out of the sergeant. If he had been assigned to the northern outposts of Gaul or Britain, he might even relate to the always-shivering winter atmosphere (perhaps literally, since in Julius Caesar's time, Roman troops crossed the Rhine into Germania). Please don't get me wrong here: it is obvious that we do not all share the same viewpoints on all things. *Hogan's Heroes* is unapologetically sexist, and the Romans apparently enjoyed watching gladiators kill each other. But much of what drives us, once we put our cultural quirks aside, is the same, because human beings, being human beings, tend to do the same things, laugh at those things, and (perhaps) learn from them as well.

It's Not About the Lute-Strings

In the past year or so, I have revisited and revised several of the earlier Plutarch studies, even those that were completed or cleaned up for publication only a few years ago; so a few of them are now on their third version. I've been doing this *not* to bring them into line with current cultural ideas, but simply to make my part of the studies better and easier to use: Plutarch, for his part, is fully capable of standing on his own. What I've noticed in my own review of those *Lives* is that they often do, without being preachy about it, show us what a mixed bag of morality most people are, but also what good things can happen when we search for valour. And not only sword-wielding valour that wins battles, but integrity-valour, in situations as minor as Eumenes' accounting for "borrowed" horses; or generosity-valour, as in King Agis's proposal that debts should be cancelled and land shared with the poor. When criticized for this, he said,

> "And you that are wont to praise Ecprepes, who,
> being ephor, cut with his hatchet two of the nine
> strings from the instrument of Phrynis the
> musician, and to commend those who afterwards
> imitated him, in cutting the strings of Timotheus's
> harp, with what face can you blame us for designing
> to cut off superfluity and luxury and display from
> the commonwealth? Do you think those men were
> so concerned only about a lute-string, or intended
> anything else than to check in music that same
> excess and extravagance which rule in our present
> lives and manners, and have disturbed and
> destroyed all the harmony and order of our city?"

There is intolerance-of-corrupt-bullying-power valour, as in the abrupt replacement of the Spartan ephors by Agis and his co-ruler Cleombrotus. But watch what happens with that one:

> "Thus far all things proceeded prosperously, none
> daring to oppose; but through the sordid weakness
> of one man, these promising beginnings were
> blasted, and a most noble and truly Spartan
> purpose overthrown and ruined by the love of
> money."

Oh, money again. Yes, we know about that.

And then there is persistence-without-pampering valour, as in this description of Agis:

> "...they saw such discipline and exact obedience
> under a leader who perhaps was the youngest man
> in all the army. They saw also how he was himself
> content to fare hardly, ready to undergo any
> labours, and not to be distinguished by pomp or
> richness of habit [dress] or arms from the meanest
> of his soldiers; and to people in general it was an
> object of regard and admiration. But rich men
> viewed the innovation with dislike and alarm, lest
> haply the example might spread, and work changes
> to their prejudice in their own countries as well."

People often don't want change, even good change, when it threatens their own status or lifestyle. Innovators and shaker-uppers risk being punished, financially or socially; or even getting killed, like Agis. Does reading *Agis and Cleomenes* make us want to settle for being a mediocre leader (and avoid getting sent to the Russian front); or take hold faithfully of whatever task has been put in front of us?

> Fight the good fight of faith, lay hold on eternal life,
> whereunto thou art also called, and hast professed a
> good profession before many witnesses. (1 Timothy
> 6:11-12)

And if we do pour out not only our material goods but our lives in the pursuit of love and justice? Well, maybe there will be someone watching or listening…or reading our stories later on. Like Cleomenes, forced by his father the king to marry the widow of Agis, who happened to be "the most youthful and beautiful woman in all Greece." But she had another important asset: she had loved Agis and remembered all his dreams and plans for Sparta. So "…[Cleomenes] would often inquire of her concerning what had passed, and attentively listen to the story of Agis's purpose and design."

Several of Plutarch's subjects are inspired by the accounts of earlier heroes, both real and (possibly) mythical.

> It is said that…after reading some part of the history
> of Alexander, he sat a great while very thoughtful,
> and at last burst out into tears. His friends were
> surprised, and asked him the reason of it. "Do you
> think," said he, "I have not just cause to weep, when
> I consider that Alexander at my age had conquered
> so many nations, and I have all this time done
> nothing that is memorable." (*Life of Julius Caesar*)

> He made Epaminondas his great example, and
> came not far behind him in activity, sagacity, and
> incorruptible integrity… (*Life of Philopoemen*)

And that is why Plutarch's *Lives* are, essentially, practical.

Part III: Studying the Study

"… two such lives as those of Cato the Censor and Alcibiades will do much to teach future generations what good or evil one man can do for his times."

(Miss R.A. Pennethorne in *The Parents' Review*)

"And here is as great an adventure as I have ever heard of, and here, if we turn back, no little impeachment of all our honours." (Reepicheep the Mouse, in *The Voyage of the Dawn Treader* by C.S. Lewis)

Studying the Study

My original plan was to show a study for one of Plutarch's shorter *Lives*, such as *Eumenes*, as it developed from the ground up, starting with the entire, unedited block of text and ending with a final set of readings and notes. However, I realized that, aside from taking up a lot of pages, including such a long chunk of public-domain text might cause publishing problems. The compromise I came up with was to show only the first lesson (Appendices A and B), except for the final version (Appendix C). If you do want to see an entire *Life of Eumenes*, it's easy to find North's or Dryden's translation online.

Which brings us to the question of choosing a suitable English translation. My usual method these days is to start with North's, clean up the spelling and the most difficult language issues, and then merge some of the text with Dryden's wherever he was clearer. Sometimes I will change a word slightly so as not to take up unnecessary space in the vocabulary lists. However, because this study is for demonstration (as well as something you can actually use), the text you're going to see here is almost 100% Dryden's version. I have avoided mixing translations and changing words, other than modernizing the spellings of some character and place names. This has the unfortunate side effect, however, of making the lists much longer than they usually are. If you're new to these studies, please don't feel you have to pre-learn or pre-teach all those words, names, and places: they're meant to be a screwdriver, not a sledgehammer.

This raises the issue of omissions for length and/or content. This study has only a few of those, and they're marked as such right from the first stage (because if I left them in, we'd have a book with adult content, also a publishing problem). *Eumenes* doesn't have much that's inappropriate, but I am trying to keep the youngest readers in mind.

I chose *Eumenes*, as I said, partly because it was short, but also because, in all the Plutarch studies I've done and in all the history I know about, I didn't remember ever hearing about Eumenes. I have a wonderfully short memory for certain things (I can re-read detective novels and not remember who did it), but it turns out that, in this case, I was right: a search of the existing AmblesideOnline Plutarch studies turned up no mention of Eumenes. Perfect, I thought: someone that I've never heard of and that probably nobody else knows either. We can start from scratch.

Well, I was half right. Eumenes might not have come across my own radar before, but it turns out that he was certainly not a nobody. He was one of the *Diadochi*, the "successors" who fought for control of Alexander the Great's empire after his premature death. Eumenes was unusual among the *Diadochi* because he wasn't a Macedonian general or bodyguard, but a Greek who had been scooped up in a talent search by Alexander's father Philip; and he worked, until he was about forty, as the royal private secretary. That first part of his life kind of swooshes by in the first lesson, and then his remaining years…all seven of them…are the focus of the rest.

I did tell you this was a short story.

It's also a very packed one, covering territory from Greece through Asia Minor and Egypt, and naming many people, some of them with similar and confusing names. You might wonder why it's even worth going into detail about some of them, for the sake of six lessons. However, for any places or people that you do examine more deeply, the payoff will be greater when you read the next *Life*, whichever that might be. Alexander was a sort of royal octopus, with tentacles spreading far across history. To give one example, his general Antigonus plays a big part in this story, but he also appears in the *Lives* of *Pyrrhus*, *Phocion*, his own son *Demetrius*, and of course *Alexander*.

For Eumenes, as for many others, the events of his life were a mixture of *context* (when and where he lived, who he interacted with, what the rulers and their armies were doing) and *character* (the values he lived by, the choices he made). The secret to studying these *Lives* seems to be creating a balance of both; understanding enough of the context while focusing mainly on character. The first Plutarch studies I wrote, years ago, were much stronger on character than they were on context; that's partly because I was often writing them a bit at a time, while I was reading them with my own daughters, and I didn't have a lot of time or energy to follow historic or linguistic rabbit trails. In a sense, that was all right: we were doing these studies for Citizenship, after all, so we didn't get too bogged down in dates and details. One can read Plutarch, as one can the Bible, without paying too much attention to the world history embedded in it.

However, as I've switched to writing each study as a unit, I've been able to add more history and geography notes, with explanations of things that Plutarch skips over. Some of these were valuable in correcting my own misperceptions and mistakes, such as numbering characters who share names (sometimes three or four in one *Life*). I've also suggested "creative narration" ideas that are not just frills and fun, but that are intended to help keep the context straight, such as having students make a colour-coded timeline for Greek leaders who lived between the Persian and the Peloponnesian Wars; and using moveable figures to show the revolving-door kings in *Agis and Cleomenes*.

In the Cards

What is the *context* of Eumenes, and how can we emphasize the important points about it while keeping the focus on his *character*? After I had worked through most of the vocabulary, but before I wrote any of the discussion questions or lesson introductions, I decided that, with this piece of drama having such a large cast, it would be a good idea to find a way to keep the major characters straight. The story contains much shifting of alliances, so something moveable (rather than drawing stick figures) would be preferred: the idea of "*Diadochi* trading cards" came to mind.

How many were we talking about? An online list I found included Craterus; Antipater; Alexander's seven bodyguards (Perdiccas, Ptolemy, Lysimachus, Peucestas, Peithon, Leonnatus); some Macedonian satraps (Antigonus, Neoptolemus, Seleucus, and Polyperchon); at least three members of the royal family; the second-generation *Diadochi* such as Cassander and Demetrius; and, finally, three non-Macedonians, including Eumenes. That would make about twenty cards; twenty-two if you want to include Philip and Alexander; plus maybe an extra one for the Silver Shields. A few of those characters are not included in this story, but they could be added if students want to keep the cards for further studies.

The rest of the instructions are given in the introductory notes for the study (Appendix C).

Putting the Story Straight

The next big job I had was, again, mostly one of *context*: I needed to re-read the story (several times) as Plutarch told it, and compare it with at least one historical summary. What were the major events, and how did one lead to another? Was there something that needed a little extra emphasis or explanation? Plutarch sometimes tosses off statements like "they engaged near the town of such and such," and you don't realize until later that he's talking about a major battle with all kinds of repercussions. The last half of *Eumenes* turned out to be a good example of this: like many wars, Eumenes' war against Antigonus was made up of several battles, but Plutarch didn't seem to care much about dividing the story into those distinct parts. It seemed important for us, however, to be able to track them, if only to avoid "Some people were fighting, somewhere" narrations; and, for myself, so that I could write clear introductions and propose reasonable discussion questions. For those reasons, I decided to include several in-text notes about what was going on.

Getting into Character

In more than one article on story-writing that I have read over the years, writers are advised to ask this question: what does your character, the protagonist, want very badly? And who or what force or character, the antagonist, is trying to keep him or her from getting it, maybe on purpose, or maybe because that person also wants something just as much? (This applies to reading literature, of course, as much as writing it.)

Here's a true story about getting things. One time when I was young, I went to a summer event, maybe a church thing but more likely a day camp. Anyway, there was a group of sweaty, crabby children, and the adult in charge had one banana frozen-thing-on-a-stick in her hand. Obviously trying to motivate some good behaviour, but not having a huge concern for fairness, she announced that since she had only one frozen-thing-on-a-stick, it would be given to one deserving child. She looked around and then pointed at me, because I was sitting so quietly. The thing was, I wasn't sitting quietly so that I would get a thing-on-a-stick; I didn't particularly like banana things-on-a-stick. And it put me in an embarrassing position: "Don't eat in front of people," my mother always said. But she also used to say, "If someone gives you a present, just take it and say thank you," so I took it, while trying to ignore the resentful stares of the others who had really wanted the thing-on-a-stick. I mean, a thing-on-a-stick isn't even like a bag of candy that you can share out. So, feeling some guilt but not seeing any practical alternative to letting the thing melt all over my dress, I ate it myself.

The big, big motivator in the story of Eumenes is political and military power. Wealth, too, but largely power: everybody in his world wanted control over kingdoms, satrapies, armies. Towards the end of Eumenes' life, things were falling into place for him to have a great deal of that power; and he wasn't very old, so he could probably have enjoyed it for years to come. However, if you look at the early career of Eumenes, he either had an incredible amount of patience and cunning to wait so long for his frozen-thing-on-a-stick, or maybe that wasn't even his original ambition. When one did fall in his lap, it turned out to have somebody else's name on it, but he couldn't exactly give it back; in fact, certain people were determined to make sure that he did get to have it. By the end of the story, it was kill-or-be-killed; but the major antagonist (or Antigonist, in this case) was less to blame than one small group who traded Eumenes for, shall we say, a whole cooler full of things-on-a-stick.

For All Practical Purposes

So was Eumenes merely a victim of circumstance? Was his life decided more by context than character? If character was important, was it positive or negative?

And what evidence do we have? Beginning with Plutarch's statements that Philip picked him out of a crowd of young men, and Alexander "esteemed him as wise and faithful," it seems to be no accident that Eumenes was deemed to be worthy of his own thing-on-a-stick. But how did he handle this piece of (seeming) good luck? Was he a good military leader and negotiator? In Charlotte Mason's terms, did he follow the Way of the Will, with an object outside of himself? Did he become too ambitious? Is he an example of what his culture (or ours) would call "virtuous?"

I'm not going to attempt to answer all those questions here. In fact, I can't, because

> ...Plutarch is like the Bible in this, that he does not label the actions of his people as good or bad but leaves the conscience and judgment of his readers to make that classification. (*Philosophy of Education*, p. 186)

Charlotte said that the function of the Will is to choose:

> ...not between things, persons, and courses of
> action, but between the ideas which these represent.
> Every choice, of course, implies a rejection of one or
> many ideas opposed to the one we choose. If we
> keep the will in abeyance, things and affairs still
> present themselves, but we *allow* instead of
> choosing. We allow a suggestion from without,
> which runs with our nature, to decide for us.
> (*Ourselves Book II,* p. 147)

In *School Education* (p. 46), Charlotte used the word "practical" to describe her philosophy of education. That is not usually the first word that comes to mind in C.M., even for those using her methods. We may have an idea that "practical" applies only to completing arithmetic worksheets and learning useful things like capital cities. But the root meaning of "practical" is more closely related to the principles of conduct, particularly as they are *acted* upon. The outcome of a practical education is to use its lessons and examples to build up one's conscience, so that wise, loving, and just decisions can be made and acted upon. The goals are, as Charlotte says in *Ourselves*, first, love, and second, justice. Or, to echo Reepicheep, adventure with honour.

What important choices did Eumenes make, what ideas did they represent, and how did he act on them? Here are five, but I'm sure you can find more.

1. In an age when too much loyalty was not only unfashionable but could prove dangerous, Eumenes demonstrated an unswerving allegiance to his (adopted) royal family. In fact, this became his personal Rubicon: choosing to take an oath of loyalty to the Macedonian kings, rather than to Antigonus (who had tempted him with a high position in his government).

2. Charlotte warned that we do our Wills a disservice when "we allow a suggestion from without, which runs with our nature, to decide for us."

   Soon after Alexander's death, Eumenes was pushed by Leonnatus to help end a rebellion in Greece. As Eumenes was friends with neither Antipater, the besieged Macedonian governor there, nor the tyrant ruler of his own city, Cardia (whom Antipater had now sent to ask for help), he used that as an excuse to keep out of the expedition. Plutarch suggests that his real reason was his mistrust of Leonnatus ("a rash, headstrong, and unsafe man"). He may have thought that Leonnatus showed poor judgment by taking too seriously a letter from Cleopatra proposing marriage. He may also have thought, probably correctly, that Leonnatus wanted not so much to rescue Antipater as to unseat him. Eumenes could have accepted the suggestions from Leonnatus (making friends with the Cardian ruler; going off to fight the Greek rebels); but he decided that he stood a better chance by throwing in his lot with Perdiccas, the head of the army and Regent of the Empire. As a result, Perdiccas made him a member of his council. Leonnatus was, unfortunately, killed in battle with the rebels.

3. When Eumenes was put in charge of guarding the Hellespont, he spent time and energy in improving his military force and, especially, in adding horses to the cavalry. Soon afterwards, he was betrayed by his supposed ally, Neoptolemus; but that preparation paid off. "Here Eumenes first found the benefit of his own foresight and contrivance, for his foot being beaten, he routed Neoptolemus with his horse, and took all his baggage; and coming up with his whole force upon the phalanx while broken and disordered in its flight, obliged the men to lay down their arms and take an oath to serve under him."

4. "From [Antipater and Craterus] had come an embassy to Eumenes, inviting him over to their side, offering to secure him in his present government and to give him additional command, both of men and of territory, with the advantage of gaining his enemy Antipater to become his friend, and keeping Craterus his friend from turning to be his enemy. To which Eumenes replied that he could not so suddenly be reconciled to his old enemy Antipater, especially at a time when he saw him use his friends like enemies, but was ready to reconcile Craterus to Perdiccas, upon any and

39

equitable terms; but in case of any aggression, he would resist the injustice to his last breath, and would rather lose his life than betray his word."

(Speaks for itself.)

5.   "Passing by Mount Ida, where there was a royal establishment of horses, Eumenes took as many as he had occasion for, and sent an account of his doing so to the overseers; at which Antipater is said to have laughed, calling it truly laudable in Eumenes thus to hold himself prepared for giving in to them (or would it be taking from them?) strict account of all matters of administration." Honesty and attention to small details had kept Eumenes employed for forty years, and he was not about to stop now.

Using the Examination Questions

In the original PNEU programmes and corresponding examination questions, there are usually one or two questions for the Form II (upper elementary) students, one for Form III (middle school), and one for Form IV.

I've written elsewhere about the value of those original exam questions to educators, how they give us a sense of what the PNEU students were expected to take away from a term's work. In the case of Plutarch's *Lives*, this can be even more important, as we want to keep the focus on the ideas of Citizenship, especially personal integrity and leadership skills ("Tell how this person handled this crisis") rather than details of history or culture ("Draw a map showing all the battles of the war").

It's also valuable to have the questions for a range of ages, and this applies to all subjects: I confess to having made my own younger students' exam questions probably harder than they had to be. "Tell about the meeting between X and Y" is more typical for Form II than is "Comment on Philopoemen's opinion of Ptolemy—'always preparing and never performing.'"

The other thing I sometimes do, especially now that I include exam questions in the studies (I didn't always), is not so much "teaching to the test" as simply making sure that whatever's going to be on the exam doesn't get overlooked during the lessons. If you know you're going to ask about the Battle of Whatever, or the Journey to Wherever, you had better make sure that those proper nouns get some exposure and repetition during the term, or you may end up with a blank page. This is where, I think, creative/alternative narrations can boost retention: if you have acted the part of a news reporter covering the Battle of Plataea, you're more likely to remember who was involved and what it was called (or at least how to pronounce it).

Because Eumenes was never part of the PNEU Plutarch cycle, at least that we know of (see Appendix D), there are no existing exam questions to draw on. What I've often done for other studies, in that case, is to use questions from other terms as models. Here is a Form II example from *Timoleon*: "Give a short account of Timoleon's expedition against the Carthaginians, or, Why did Timoleon first save his brother's life and then consent to his death? Tell the whole story." The more difficult *Timoleon* questions are as follows:

> 1: (Middle school) Show how Timoleon demonstrated wisdom in his dealings with the Syracusans. How did the people back in Corinth help? How did the Syracusans reward Timoleon?

> 2: (High school) Explain the strategy that Timoleon planned to use against the Carthaginians. How did he show strong leadership, especially in dealing with the problem of the chariots? *OR* Plutarch says that Timoleon, in his last years, "neither did make himself to be envied of the citizens." What did he mean, and what would have been the dangers of doing this?

You can see how I adapted them for *Eumenes* at the end of the study guide.

And now we move on to the study as it developed, plus a look at the PNEU and AmblesideOnline coverage of the *Lives*. I wish you adventure and honour with Plutarch, and also some "fun that is funny."

Appendix A: *Life of Eumenes*, Lesson One (Unedited)

Duris reports that Eumenes, the Cardian, was the son of a poor wagoner in the Thracian Chersonesus, yet liberally educated, both as a scholar and a soldier; and that while he was but young, Philip, passing through Cardia, diverted himself with a sight of the wrestling matches and other exercises of the youth of that place, among whom Eumenes performing with success, and showing signs of intelligence and bravery, Philip was so pleased with him as to take him into his service. But they seem to speak more probably who tell us that Philip advanced Eumenes for the friendship he bore to his father, whose guest he had sometime been. After the death of Philip, he continued in the service of Alexander, with the title of his principal secretary, but in as great favour as the most intimate of his familiars, being esteemed as wise and faithful as any person about him, so that he went with troops under his immediate command as general in the expedition against India, and succeeded to the post of Perdiccas, when Perdiccas was advanced to that of Hephaestion, then newly deceased. And therefore, after the death of Alexander, when Neoptolemus, who had been captain of his life-guard, said that he had followed Alexander with shield and spear, but Eumenes only with pen and paper, the Macedonians laughed at him, as knowing very well that, besides other marks of favour, the king had done him the honour to make him a kind of kinsman to himself by marriage *[omission]*.

Notwithstanding, he frequently incurred Alexander's displeasure, and put himself into some danger, through Hephaestion. The quarters that had been taken up for Eumenes, Hephaestion assigned to Euius, the flute-player. Upon which, in great anger, Eumenes and Mentor came to Alexander and loudly complained, saying that the way to be regarded was to throw away their arms and turn flute-players or tragedians; so much so that Alexander took their part and chid Hephaestion; but soon after changed his mind again, and was angry with Eumenes, and accounted the freedom he had taken to be rather an affront to the king than a reflection upon Hephaestion. Afterwards, when Nearchus, with a fleet, was to be sent to the Southern Sea, Alexander borrowed money of his friends, his own treasury being exhausted, and would have had three hundred talents of Eumenes, but he sent a hundred only, pretending that it was not without great difficulty he had raised so much from his stewards. Alexander neither complained nor took the money, but gave private orders to set Eumenes's tent on fire, designing to take him in a manifest lie, when his money was carried out. But before that could be done the tent was consumed, and Alexander repented of his orders, all his papers being burnt; the gold and silver, however, which was melted down in the fire, being afterwards collected, was found to be more than one thousand talents; yet Alexander took none of it, and only wrote to the several governors and generals to send new copies of the papers that were burnt, and ordered them to be delivered to Eumenes.

Another difference happened between him and Hephaestion concerning a gift, and a great deal of ill language passed between them, yet Eumenes still continued in favour. But Hephaestion dying soon after, the king, in his grief, presuming all those that differed with Hephaestion in his lifetime were now rejoicing at his death, showed much harshness and severity in his behaviour with them, especially towards Eumenes, whom he often upbraided with his quarrels and ill language to Hephaestion. But he, being a wise and dexterous courtier, made advantage of what had done him prejudice, and struck in with the king's passion for glorifying his friend's memory, suggesting various plans to do him honour, and contributing largely and readily towards erecting his monument.

After Alexander's death, when the quarrel broke out between the troops of the phalanx and the officers, his companions, Eumenes, though in his judgment he inclined to the latter, yet in his professions stood neuter, as if he thought it unbecoming him, who was a stranger, to interpose in the private quarrels of the Macedonians. When the rest of Alexander's friends left Babylon, he stayed behind, and did much to pacify the foot-soldiers, and to dispose them towards an accommodation. And when the officers had agreed among themselves, and, recovering from the first disorder proceeded to share out the several commands and provinces, they made Eumenes governor of Cappadocia and Paphlagonia, and all the coast upon the Pontic Sea as far as Trebizond, which at that time was not subject to the Macedonians, for Ariarathes kept it as king, but Leonnatus and

Antigonus, with a large army, were to put him in possession of it.

Antigonus, already filled with hopes of his own, and despising all men, took no notice of Perdiccas's letter; but Leonnatus with his army came down into Phrygia to the service of Eumenes. But being visited by Hecataeus, the tyrant of the Cardians, and requested rather to relieve Antipater and the Macedonians that were besieged in Lamia, he resolved upon that expedition, inviting Eumenes to a share in it, and endeavouring to reconcile him to Hecataeus. For there was an hereditary feud between them, arising out of political differences, and Eumenes had more than once been known to denounce Hecataeus as a tyrant, and to exhort Alexander to restore the Cardians their liberty. Therefore at this time, also, he declined the expedition proposed, pretending that he feared lest Antipater, who already hated him, should for that reason, and to gratify Hecataeus, kill him. Leonnatus so far believed as to impart to Eumenes his whole design, which, as he had pretended and given out, was to aid Antipater, but in truth was to seize the kingdom of Macedon; and he showed him letters from Cleopatra, in which, it appeared, she invited him to Pella, with promises to marry him. But Eumenes, whether fearing Antipater, or looking upon Leonnatus as a rash, headstrong, and unsafe man, stole away from him by night, taking with him all his men, namely, three hundred horse, and two hundred of his own servants armed, and all his gold, to the value of five thousand talents of silver, and fled to Perdiccas, discovered to him Leonnatus's design, and thus gained great interest with him, and was made of the council. Soon after, Perdiccas, with a great army, which he led himself, conducted Eumenes into Cappadocia, and, having taken Ariarathes prisoner, and subdued the whole country, declared him governor of it. He accordingly proceeded to dispose of the chief cities among his own friends, and made captains of garrisons, judges, receivers, and other officers, of such as he thought fit himself, Perdiccas not at all interposing. Eumenes, however, still continued to attend upon Perdiccas, both out of respect to him, and a desire not to be absent from the royal family.

But Perdiccas, believing he was able enough to attain his own further objects without assistance, and that the country he left behind him might stand in need of an active and faithful governor, when he came into Cilicia dismissed Eumenes, under colour of sending him to his command, but in truth to secure Armenia, which was on its frontier, and was unsettled through the practices of Neoptolemus. Him, a proud and vain man, Eumenes exerted himself to gain by personal attentions; but to balance the Macedonian foot, whom he found insolent and self-willed, he contrived to raise an army of horse, excusing from tax and contribution all those of the country that were able to serve on horseback, and buying up a number of horses, which he distributed among such of his own men as he most confided in, stimulating the courage of his new soldiers by gifts and honours, and inuring their bodies to service by frequent marching and exercising; so that the Macedonians were some of them astonished, others overjoyed to see that in so short a time he had got together a body of no less than six thousand three hundred horsemen.

Appendix B: *Life of Eumenes*, Lesson One (First Draft)

My copy of Dryden's Plutarch says that Eumenes "Reigned 197?—160 B.C." When I first read that, I wondered what was happening in the world in that century, who Eumenes was (a king?), and where he lived. I read through the first section of Dryden's text, somewhat puzzled by the Macedonian references, and jotted down some questions. Then I went and looked up the background information.

How This is an Example of Having to Verify Everything Yourself: The dates in my copy of Plutarch are **wrong**: they refer to Eumenes II, a later ruler of Pergamon. The Eumenes we have here is **Eumenes of Cardia**, who lived from c. 362 B.C.-316 B.C. Please note that the rest of my comments in this first pass through Eumenes' story were made before correcting that information.

Vocabulary

wagoner: some sort of delivery person?

liberally educated: well educated in many subjects, with a broad perspective on things (Is this going to be important later on?)

the most intimate of his familiars: his closest friends

to be regarded: to get respect

chid: scolded, reproved

affront: insult, source of displeasure

talents: the weight of a talent could vary, but even one talent was a large sum of money

upbraided: same as **chid**

dexterous: The U.S. spelling of **dextrous**, meaning skillful

what had done him prejudice: what had counted against him

troops of the phalanx: The word **phalanx** is a clear indicator that we are talking about the Macedonian army.

in his professions stood neuter: he refused to make a public statement about his position

dispose them towards an accommodation: encourage them to settle the dispute

discovered to him: told him

was made of the council: which council are we talking about?

dispose of the chief cities among his own friends: made his friends rulers of those places

interposing: interfering

inuring: hardening, accustoming

People

Philip: the king of Macedonia? Which one?

Alexander: son of Philip

Perdiccas

Hephaestion

Neoptolemus

Artabazus

Euius, the flute-player: Do we know any more than this about him?

Mentor

Nearchus

Ariarathes

Leonnatus and Antigonus: Familiar names!

Hecataeus

Antipater

Cleopatra: which one?

Historic Occasions

the expedition against India: When was this? Are we talking about Alexander the Great? That doesn't fit with the dates given.

After Alexander's death: When was this?

When the rest of Alexander's friends left Babylon: And this?

On the Map

Cardia (Cardians): Where Eumenes came from

Thracian Chersonesus: his birthplace

Macedon (Macedonians)

Southern Sea: which one?

Cappadocia and Paphlagonia: These sound Biblical.

Trebizond

Phrygia

Lamia

Pella

Cilicia

Armenia

Reading

Part One

Duris reports that Eumenes, the Cardian, was the son of a poor

wagoner in the **Thracian Chersonesus**, yet **liberally educated**, both as a scholar and a soldier; and that while he was but young, **Philip**, passing through Cardia, diverted himself with a sight of the wrestling matches and other exercises of the youth of that place, among whom Eumenes performing with success, and showing signs of intelligence and bravery, Philip was so pleased with him as to take him into his service. But they seem to speak more probably who tell us that Philip advanced Eumenes for the friendship he bore to his father, whose guest he had sometime been. After the death of Philip, he continued in the service of **Alexander**, with the title of his principal secretary, but in as great favour as **the most intimate of his familiars**, being esteemed as wise and faithful as any person about him, so that he went with troops under his immediate command as general in **the expedition against India**, and succeeded to the post of **Perdiccas**, when Perdiccas was advanced to that of **Hephaestion**, then newly deceased. And therefore, after the death of Alexander, when **Neoptolemus**, who had been captain of his life-guard, said that he had followed Alexander with shield and spear, but Eumenes only with pen and paper, the **Macedonians** laughed at him, as knowing very well that, besides other marks of favour, the king had done him the honour to make him a kind of kinsman to himself by marriage [omission].

Notwithstanding, he frequently incurred Alexander's displeasure, and put himself into some danger, through Hephaestion. The quarters that had been taken up for Eumenes, Hephaestion assigned to **Euius, the flute-player**. Upon which, in great anger, Eumenes and **Mentor** came to Alexander and loudly complained, saying that the way **to be regarded** was to throw away their arms and turn flute-players or tragedians; so much so that Alexander took their part and **chid** Hephaestion; but soon after changed his mind again, and was angry with Eumenes, and accounted the freedom he had taken to be rather an **affront** to the king than a reflection upon Hephaestion. Afterwards, when **Nearchus**, with a fleet, was to be sent to the **Southern Sea**, Alexander borrowed money of his friends, his own treasury being exhausted, and would have had three hundred **talents** of Eumenes, but he sent a hundred only, pretending that it was not without great difficulty he had raised so much from his stewards. Alexander neither complained nor took the money, but gave private orders to set **Eumenes's** tent on fire, designing to take him in a manifest lie, when his money was carried out. But before that could be done the tent was consumed, and Alexander repented of his orders, all his papers being burnt; the gold and silver, however, which was melted down in the fire, being afterwards collected, was found to be more than one thousand talents; yet Alexander took none of it, and only wrote to the several governors and generals to send new copies of the papers that were burnt, and ordered them to be delivered to Eumenes.

Part Two (Do we need a Part Two?)

Another difference happened between him and Hephaestion concerning a gift, and a great deal of ill language passed between them, yet Eumenes still continued in favour. But Hephaestion dying soon after, the king, in his grief, presuming all those that differed with Hephaestion in his lifetime were now rejoicing at his death, showed much harshness and severity in his behaviour with them, especially towards Eumenes, whom he often **upbraided** with his quarrels and ill language to Hephaestion. But he, being a wise and **dexterous** courtier, made advantage of **what had done him prejudice**, and struck in with the king's passion for glorifying his friend's memory, suggesting various plans to do him honour, and contributing largely and readily towards erecting his monument.

Part Three

After Alexander's death, when the quarrel broke out between the **troops of the phalanx** and the officers, his companions, Eumenes, though in his judgment he inclined to the latter, yet **in his professions stood neuter**, as if he thought it unbecoming him, who was a stranger, to interpose in the private quarrels of the Macedonians. **When the rest of Alexander's friends left Babylon**, he stayed behind, and did much to pacify the foot-soldiers, and to **dispose them towards an accommodation**. And when the officers had agreed among themselves, and, recovering from the first disorder proceeded to share out the several commands and provinces, they made Eumenes governor of **Cappadocia and Paphlagonia**, and all the coast upon the Pontic Sea as far as **Trebizond**, which at that time was not subject to the Macedonians, for **Ariarathes** kept it as king, but **Leonnatus and Antigonus**, with a large army, were to put him in possession of it.

Part Four

Antigonus, already filled with hopes of his own, and despising all men, took no notice of **Perdiccas's** letter; but Leonnatus with his army came down into **Phrygia** to the service of Eumenes. But being visited by **Hecataeus**, the tyrant of the Cardians, and requested rather to relieve **Antipater** and the Macedonians that were besieged in **Lamia**, he resolved upon that expedition, inviting Eumenes to a share in it, and endeavouring to reconcile him to Hecataeus. For there was an hereditary feud between them, arising out of political differences, and Eumenes had more than once been known to denounce Hecataeus as a tyrant, and to exhort Alexander to restore the Cardians their liberty. Therefore at this time, also, he declined the expedition proposed, pretending that he feared lest Antipater, who already hated him, should for that reason, and to gratify Hecataeus, kill him. Leonnatus so far believed as to impart to Eumenes his whole design, which, as he had pretended and given out, was to aid Antipater, but in truth was to seize the kingdom of Macedon; and he showed him letters from **Cleopatra**, in which, it appeared, she invited him to **Pella**, with promises to marry him. But Eumenes, whether fearing Antipater, or looking upon Leonnatus as a rash, headstrong, and unsafe man, stole away from him by night, taking with him all his men, namely, three hundred horse, and two hundred of his own servants armed, and all his gold, to the value of five thousand talents of silver, and fled to Perdiccas, **discovered to him** Leonnatus's design, and thus gained great interest with him, and **was made of the council**. Soon after, Perdiccas, with a great army, which he led himself, conducted Eumenes into Cappadocia, and, having taken Ariarathes prisoner, and subdued the whole country, declared him governor of it. He accordingly proceeded to **dispose of the chief cities among his own friends**, and made captains of garrisons, judges, receivers, and other officers, of such as he thought fit himself, Perdiccas not at all **interposing**. Eumenes, however, still continued to attend upon

Perdiccas, both out of respect to him, and a desire not to be absent from the royal family.

But Perdiccas, believing he was able enough to attain his own further objects without assistance, and that the country he left behind him might stand in need of an active and faithful governor, when he came into **Cilicia** dismissed Eumenes, under colour of sending him to his command, but in truth to secure **Armenia**, which was on its frontier, and was unsettled through the practices of Neoptolemus. Him, a proud and vain man, Eumenes exerted himself to gain by personal attentions; but to balance the Macedonian foot, whom he found insolent and self-willed, he contrived to raise an army of horse, excusing from tax and contribution all those of the country that were able to serve on horseback, and buying up a number of horses, which he distributed among such of his own men as he most confided in, stimulating the courage of his new soldiers by gifts and honours, and **inuring** their bodies to service by frequent marching and exercising; so that the Macedonians were some of them astonished, others overjoyed to see that in so short a time he had got together a body of no less than six thousand three hundred horsemen.

Appendix C: *Life of Eumenes,* Complete Study Guide

Eumenes of Cardia was one of the *Diadochi*: the friends, relatives, and military colleagues of Alexander the Great, who were left, after his sudden death, to parcel out the pieces of his empire among themselves. Eumenes was unusual among the *Diadochi* because he wasn't a Macedonian general or bodyguard, but a Greek who had been recruited as a young man by Philip, the king of Macedon.

Who were Philip and Alexander?

For many years, the dominant political power in Europe and the Middle East had been the Persian empire; but Persia's strength had weakened, and its subjects were becoming rebellious. **Philip II of Macedon** was credited with reforming and strengthening the Macedonian army (using the famous phalanx formation). He planned to combine Macedon's military power with that of the Greek states, and to attack Persia.

Philip's assassination in 336 left that ambition unfulfilled. However, his son Alexander ("The Great") spent the next thirteen years conquering a previously undreamed-of share of the world.

Is it Macedon or Macedonia? Were the Macedonians Greeks?

The names are used interchangeably. Macedonia, or Macedon, was a kingdom in the northeastern part of mainland Greece. The Macedonians were Greek in many respects, such as religious beliefs; but they valued their distinct heritage and identity.

What were The Wars of the Diadochi?

The Greek word *Diadochi* (pronounced dye-AD-a-kee) means "successors." It refers to the of Alexander who battled for control of his empire after his sudden death. The Wars of the Diadochi lasted from 322 until 281 B.C.

The Kings of Macedon

King Philip II of Macedon was succeeded by his son Alexander III (The Great). But what happened after that?

Alexander died without a clear heir to his throne, although his wife was expecting a child. His older half-brother Arrhidaeus became king (he was officially called Philip III), but due to a disability he was unable to rule completely, so most of the decisions were made by regents: Perdiccas, then Antipater, and finally Polyperchon. Antipater's decision to name General Polyperchon as the next regent, instead of his son Cassander, caused an ugly power struggle.

The son born after Alexander's death also had people who supported his right to the throne over that of his uncle; and after Philip III was put to death in 317 B.C., he became King Alexander IV, and "ruled" until he was murdered in 310 or 309 B.C.

And what about Cassander, the son of Antipater? He essentially ruled Macedon from 317 B.C. until he was formally made king in 305. (He died in 297 B.C.)

Who or what were the Silver Shields?

The Silver Shields were a hand-picked, highly skilled division of the Macedonian army, who had served under Alexander; they later helped Eumenes in his battles against Antigonus. By the time of this story, they were getting on a bit in years, but they were still mighty and feared. Their Greek name, which you will see used in older translations, is the *Argyraspides* (sometimes spelled *Argyraspids*).

Did Eumenes have a family?

Eumenes was married to Artonis, the daughter of Artabazus II, a Persian general who was satrap of Phrygia. Her sister Barsine had been romantically involved with Alexander the Great, so Alexander's "suggestion" of Artonis as a wife for Eumenes was a mark of his favour; even, as Plutarch suggests, a way of creating kinship.

We don't know about specific children, but they are mentioned in the last lesson.

Appendix C

Creating Character Cards

As a storytelling and narration tool for this study, I recommend making a set of *Diadochi* character cards, similar to trading cards. They can be as simple or as fancy as you like, especially when it comes to adding portraits (optional). The whole set of cards could be created at the beginning of the study, with names and colour-coding, adding details later; *or* you might begin with those mentioned in the first lesson, and add on as you go. In that case, you will not have a complete set by the end of the study, as some of the *Diadochi* are not named here (Lysimachus, Peithon, Seleucus, and Pyrrhus). The cards can be saved and referred to later on in other Plutarch or history studies; if you create them as you go, you could add the other characters when they come up at other times. If you are working with a small group, you might decide to make one set of cards for everyone.

What you will need: Fifteen to twenty index cards, or half-cards if you prefer. (If you want to include character cards for Philip and Alexander, that will bring the total to twenty-two; two cards for the leaders of the Silver Shields would make twenty-four.) Coloured pens and/or markers to write with and decorate the cards.

The list of characters: Craterus and Antipater have individual cards. Alexander's bodyguards (Perdiccas, Ptolemy I Soter, Lysimachus, Peucestas, Peithon, Leonnatus) have cards with the same coloured border, or a symbol that shows their connection. The group of four Macedonian satraps (Antigonus, Neoptolemus, Seleucus, and Polyperchon) should also share a colour or symbol; also for members of the royal family (Alexander's sister Cleopatra; his son Alexander IV; and his half-brother Arrhidaeus/Philip III); two of the second-generation *Diadochi*, Cassander and Demetrius; and, finally, the non-Macedonian *Diadochi*, including Pyrrhus of Epirus and Eumenes. Optional additions to the royal family group would be Olympias, the mother of Alexander; and Roxana, his wife. Finally, you might add either one card to represent all the Silver Shields, or one card each for the two commanders, Antigenes and Teutamus.

What to put on the cards: Name (and pronunciation, if helpful);

country of origin; position or rank. Optional: successes/failures; best friend/worst enemy; "superpower." It might be a good idea to note the three regents of Alexander's empire: Perdiccas, Antipater, and Polyperchon.

Top Vocabulary Terms

If you are familiar with these words and phrases, you will be well on the way to mastering the vocabulary for the *Life of Eumenes*. They will not be included in the lessons.

1. **baggage:** any of the equipment or supplies, such as food and weapons, belonging to a troop of soldiers. In **Lessons Five** and **Six**, the "baggage" described belonged to the Silver Shields (see the note above), and it included their family members plus years' worth of collected **spoils** (see below).

2. **barbarians:** In this story, "barbarians" refers to any people outside of the Greek and Macedonian cultures, but mainly to those of the former Persian Empire.

3. **corn:** grain, such as wheat or barley

4. **design:** plot, scheme (can be either a noun or a verb). **Practise** often means the same thing.

5. **fly:** flee, escape

6. **foot:** foot-soldiers, or infantry. Cavalry, or soldiers on horseback, are often called just **horse**.

7. **garrison:** a place where soldiers are stationed, or it can also mean the soldiers themselves

8. **phalanx:** the Macedonian battle formation, formed by soldiers standing close together so that their shields acted as one large shield, with their spears out like the quills on a porcupine

9. **satrap:** governor (a term used in the Persian Empire). A **satrapy** was a region within the empire.

10. **spoil, spoils**: Treasure or loot taken from an enemy or from a captured city. Also called **booty**.

11. **talent:** a certain amount of gold or silver, regarded as a unit of money. The exact weight varied (depending on time and place), but even one talent was always a large sum of money.

A logistics note for teachers and facilitators: Some of these lessons are quite long, though (aside from the vocabulary lists) no more so than other Plutarch Project studies. Still, some people prefer to read slowly and not complete a whole lesson in one sitting. The readings are broken up into sections to make this easier.

Lesson One

Introduction

Eumenes, for about the first forty years of his life, had a relatively safe and uneventful career...that is, about as safe and uneventful as possible when one is private secretary to two nation-conquering Macedonian kings. He was promoted to general during Alexander's time in India, and later took on the responsibilities Perdiccas had formerly held; but he was still regarded by many as a pencil-pusher.

However, Eumenes' world was turned upside-down with the death of Alexander. The rest of the royal family, the Macedonian generals, and even Alexander's bodyguards all began to fight for a piece of his huge empire. Eumenes, because of his administrative skills and loyalty to the royal family, was offered the governorship of two territories in Asia Minor. (A slight problem was that the ruler there wasn't quite ready to give it up.)

Vocabulary

wagoner: one who transports goods

liberally educated: well educated in many subjects

57

the most intimate of his familiars: his closest friends

to be regarded: to get respect

tragedians: actors

chid: scolded, reproved

affront: insult, source of displeasure

would have had: wanted, demanded

designing to take him in a manifest lie…: If Eumenes was caught trying to rescue his money from the fire, it would prove that he had more on hand than he claimed.

upbraided: same as **chid**

dexterous: or **dextrous**; skillful

what had done him prejudice: what had counted against him

troops of the phalanx: foot-soldiers

in his professions stood neuter: he refused to make a public statement about his position

dispose them towards an accommodation: encourage them to settle the dispute

Perdiccas's letter: the order for him to go and assist Eumenes

denounce: declare to be wrong

fled to Perdiccas: Perdiccas was acting as regent of Alexander's empire, with headquarters in Babylon

discovered to him: told him

interposing: interfering

still continued to attend upon Perdiccas: continued to assist Perdiccas in running the empire from Babylon

in truth to secure Armenia: Eumenes was sent not only to govern his own territory, but to keep an eye on the somewhat untrustworthy Neoptolemus next door.

frontier: border, boundary

insolent: arrogant, rude

most confided in: trusted most

inuring: hardening, accustoming

People

Duris: or Douris; the author of a book of Greek and Macedonian history which has since been lost

Philip, Alexander: see introductory notes

Perdiccas: a Macedonian general, later the head of the Imperial Army, and one of Alexander's seven bodyguards. He served as regent during the reign of Alexander's half-brother Arrhidaeus. (**Arrhidaeus** became King Philip III of Macedon; but according to historians, he was not considered fully capable of ruling, possibly due to a childhood injury.)

Hephaestion: one of Alexander's closest friends

Neoptolemus: an officer under Alexander

Mentor: a Greek mercenary soldier who became the satrap of the Asiatic coast.

Nearchus: or Nearchos; Alexander's chief admiral and official explorer. He is not counted among the official *Diadochi*, although he did continue to serve and advise Antigonus and his son Demetrius.

Ariarathes: the ruler of Cappadocia

Leonnatus: one of Alexander's bodyguards

Antigonus: Antigonus Monopthalmus (or "Antigonus with One Eye"), one of Alexander's top generals

Hecataeus: a friend of Alexander, who was made ruler of Cardia

Antipater: or Antipatros. An advisor and friend to Alexander during the early years of his reign; he acted as regent (substitute ruler) when Alexander was in Persia and India. In the last year of his life, he became regent again.

Cleopatra: Cleopatra of Macedon, the sister of Alexander

Historic Occasions

c. 400 B.C.: Birth of Antipater

c. 390-380 B.C.: Birth of Polyperchon

c. 382 B.C.: Birth of Antigonus

c. 370 B.C.: Birth of Craterus

c. 362 B.C.: Birth of Eumenes

357 B.C.: Athens took control of Chersonesus (Eumenes' home territory)

356 B.C.: Birth of Alexander the Great

336 B.C.: Death of Philip II of Macedon; accession of Alexander

334 B.C.: Alexander began his invasion of the Persian empire

327 B.C.: Alexander began his campaign in India

323 B.C.: Death of Alexander

323-322 B.C.: The Lamian War, in which Athens and its allies fought Macedon and Boeotia for control of Greece.

323-319 B.C.: Eumenes was made satrap of Cappadocia and Paphlagonia; however, Cappadocia had never been completely conquered by Alexander, and Ariarathes (a satrap who now ruled as king there) was not willing to give it up. Leonnatus was ordered to go and force Ariarathes to surrender, but he went to Macedonia instead.

Spring of 322 B.C.: Perdiccas (no doubt saying "if you want anything done you have to do it yourself") marched into Cappadocia to reassert the rule of Macedonia there.

Summer of 322 B.C.: Ariarathes was defeated and put to death by Perdiccas, enabling Eumenes to govern without interference.

On the Map

As an introduction to this study, students should have access to a map showing the Macedonian empire under Alexander the Great. Students who have not yet read much about Alexander should know he was able to conquer an unheard-of amount of territory in only a few years, including the extremely powerful Persian empire; but that his unexpected death left all those countries and kingdoms either fighting to regain their independence (such as Greece), or as prizes to be fought over by his successors.

It would also be worthwhile, in this lesson or the next, to talk about Plutarch's terms **Asia** and **Asia Minor**: what did that mean in the ancient world? (Christian students may want to look for references to Asia in the New Testament, e.g. Acts 2:9, Acts 19:10, Romans 16:5, Revelation 1:4). What is the **Hellespont**?

Thrace: a region of southeastern Europe which includes parts of present-day Greece, Turkey, and Bulgaria.

Chersonesus: or Chersonese. A Greek colony on the shores of the Black Sea. **Cardia** was its chief town.

Macedon (Macedonians): see introductory notes

Southern Sea: This was a major voyage to the **Persian Gulf** (you can find out more about it if you look up **Nearchus**)

Babylon: the capital city of the ancient Babylonian empire, which had been captured by Alexander

Cappadocia: a region of central **Anatolia** (now part of **Turkey**)

Paphlagonia: a region on the coast of the **Pontic** or **Black Sea**

Trebizond: or Trabzon; a city on the Black Sea

Phrygia: a kingdom (or satrapy) in Anatolia

Lamia: a city in central Greece. The Greeks were rebelling against Macedonian rule, and the governor there, **Antipater**, had shut himself behind the walls of the city for protection.

Pella: the Macedonian capital city

Cilicia: a region within the Persian empire, part of present-day Turkey

Armenia: a kingdom of western **Asia**

Reading

Part One

Duris reports that Eumenes, the **Cardian**, was the son of a poor **wagoner** in the **Thracian Chersonesus**, yet **liberally educated**, both as a scholar and a soldier; and that while he was but young, **Philip**, passing through Cardia, diverted himself with a sight of the wrestling matches and other exercises of the youth of that place, among whom Eumenes performing with success, and showing signs of intelligence and bravery, Philip was so pleased with him as to take him into his service. But they seem to speak more probably who tell us that Philip advanced Eumenes for the friendship he bore to his father, whose guest he had sometime been.

After the death of Philip, he continued in the service of **Alexander**, with the title of his principal secretary, but in as great favour as **the most intimate of his familiars**, being esteemed as wise and faithful as any person about him, so that he went with troops under his immediate command as general in **the expedition against India**, and succeeded to the post of **Perdiccas**, when Perdiccas was advanced to that of **Hephaestion**, then newly deceased. And therefore, after the death of Alexander, when **Neoptolemus**, who had been captain of his life-guard, said that he had followed Alexander with shield and spear, but Eumenes only with pen and paper, the **Macedonians** laughed at him, as knowing very well that, besides other marks of favour, the king had done him the honour to make him a kind of kinsman to himself by marriage *[omission]*.

Notwithstanding, he frequently incurred Alexander's displeasure, and put himself into some danger, through Hephaestion. The quarters that had been taken up for Eumenes, Hephaestion assigned to Euius, the flute-player. Upon which, in great anger,

Eumenes and **Mentor** came to Alexander and loudly complained, saying that the way **to be regarded** was to throw away their arms and turn flute-players or **tragedians**; so much so that Alexander took their part and **chid** Hephaestion; but soon after changed his mind again, and was angry with Eumenes, and accounted the freedom he had taken to be rather an **affront** to the king than a reflection upon Hephaestion.

Afterwards, when **Nearchus**, with a fleet, was to be sent to the **Southern Sea**, Alexander borrowed money of his friends, his own treasury being exhausted, and **would have had** three hundred talents of Eumenes, but he sent a hundred only, pretending that it was not without great difficulty he had raised so much from his stewards. Alexander neither complained nor took the money, but gave private orders to set Eumenes' tent on fire, **designing to take him in a manifest lie, when his money was carried out**. But before that could be done the tent was consumed, and Alexander repented of his orders, all his papers being burnt; the gold and silver, however, which was melted down in the fire, being afterwards collected, was found to be more than one thousand talents; yet Alexander took none of it, and only wrote to the several governors and generals to send new copies of the papers that were burnt, and ordered them to be delivered to Eumenes.

Another difference happened between him and Hephaestion concerning a gift, and a great deal of ill language passed between them, yet Eumenes still continued in favour. But Hephaestion dying soon after, the king, in his grief, presuming all those that differed with Hephaestion in his lifetime were now rejoicing at his death, showed much harshness and severity in his behaviour with them, especially towards Eumenes, whom he often **upbraided** with his quarrels and ill language to Hephaestion. But he, being a wise and **dexterous** courtier, made advantage of **what had done him prejudice**, and struck in with the king's passion for glorifying his friend's memory, suggesting various plans to do him honour, and contributing largely and readily towards erecting his monument.

Part Two

After Alexander's death, when the quarrel broke out between the **troops of the phalanx** and the officers, [Alexander's] companions,

Eumenes, though in his judgment he inclined to the latter, yet **in his professions stood neuter**, as if he thought it unbecoming him, who was a stranger, to interpose in the private quarrels of the Macedonians. When the rest of Alexander's friends left **Babylon**, he stayed behind, and did much to pacify the foot-soldiers, and to **dispose them towards an accommodation**. And when the officers had agreed among themselves, and, recovering from the first disorder proceeded to share out the several commands and provinces, they made Eumenes governor of **Cappadocia** and **Paphlagonia**, and all the coast upon the **Pontic Sea** as far as **Trebizond**, which at that time was not subject to the Macedonians, for **Ariarathes** kept it as king, but **Leonnatus** and **Antigonus**, with a large army, were to put him in possession of it.

Part Three

Antigonus, already filled with hopes of his own, and despising all men, took no notice of **Perdiccas's letter**; but Leonnatus with his army came down into **Phrygia** to the service of Eumenes. But (Leonnatus) being visited by **Hecataeus**, the tyrant of the Cardians, and requested rather to relieve **Antipater** and the Macedonians that were besieged in **Lamia**, he resolved upon that expedition, inviting Eumenes to a share in it, and endeavouring to reconcile him to Hecataeus. For there was an hereditary feud between them, arising out of political differences, and Eumenes had more than once been known to **denounce** Hecataeus as a tyrant, and to exhort Alexander to restore the Cardians their liberty. Therefore at this time, also, he declined the expedition proposed, pretending that he feared lest Antipater, who already hated him, should for that reason, and to gratify Hecataeus, kill him.

Leonnatus so far believed as to impart to Eumenes his whole design, which, as he had pretended and given out, was to aid Antipater, but in truth was to seize the kingdom of Macedon; and he showed him letters from **Cleopatra**, in which, it appeared, she invited him to **Pella**, with promises to marry him. But Eumenes, whether fearing Antipater, or looking upon Leonnatus as a rash, headstrong, and unsafe man, stole away from him by night, taking with him all his men, namely, three hundred horse, and two hundred of his own servants armed, and all his gold, to the value of five thousand talents of silver, and **fled to Perdiccas**, **discovered to him** Leonnatus's design, and thus gained great interest with him, and was made of the council.

Part Four

Soon after, Perdiccas, with a great army, which he led himself, conducted Eumenes into Cappadocia, and, having taken Ariarathes prisoner, and subdued the whole country, declared him governor of it. He (Eumenes) accordingly proceeded to dispose of the chief cities among his own friends, and made captains of garrisons, judges, receivers, and other officers, of such as he thought fit himself, Perdiccas not at all **interposing**. Eumenes, however, **still continued to attend upon Perdiccas**, both out of respect to him, and a desire not to be absent from the royal family.

But Perdiccas, believing he was able enough to attain his own further objects without assistance, and that the country he left behind him might stand in need of an active and faithful governor, when he came into Cilicia dismissed Eumenes, under colour of sending him to his command, but **in truth to secure Armenia**, which was on its **frontier**, and was unsettled through the practices of Neoptolemus. Him, a proud and vain man, Eumenes exerted himself to gain by personal attentions; but to balance the Macedonian foot, whom he found **insolent** and self-willed, he contrived to raise an army of horse, excusing from tax and contribution all those of the country that were able to serve on horseback, and buying up a number of horses, which he distributed among such of his own men as he **most confided in**, stimulating the courage of his new soldiers by gifts and honours, and **inuring** their bodies to service by frequent marching and exercising; so that the Macedonians were some of them astonished, others overjoyed to see that in so short a time he had got together a body of no less than six thousand three hundred horsemen.

Narration and Discussion

What do you know about Eumenes so far? What impressions do you have of his early life working for Alexander?

Using the character cards you are creating, retell the story of how Eumenes was finally put in office in Cappadocia.

At the end of the lesson, we read that Eumenes was increasing his military force in Cappadocia, buying war horses from the locals, and trying to improve the motivation and loyalty of the Macedonian soldiers. Why do you think he wanted a stronger army?

Character Cards (see introductory notes): Eumenes; Perdiccas, Neoptolemus, Leonnatus, Antigonus, Antipater, Cleopatra (optional). Remember that these are the *Diadochi* only; students may want to make cards for other characters such as Philip and Alexander, or King Ariarathes.

Creative narration: Acting as a television or newspaper reporter, create a feature story called "Clerk to Commander: Exclusive Interview with Eumenes." This could also be done in written format.

Lesson Two

Introduction

The cavalry troops commanded by Eumenes were needed to help prevent rival Macedonian forces (led by Craterus and Antipater) from crossing the **Hellespont** and invading **Asia**. There was not a strong enough army in place to fight a major battle against them if they did get across, so it was vital to keep them out in the first place. As a backup plan, Perdiccas, who had gone on to fight **Ptolemy** in Egypt, would finish things up quickly there and then return to chase down the invaders.

However, it isn't Perdiccas who takes center stage here, but Craterus, Alexander's general who apparently was respected and loved by all the Macedonians, no matter what side they currently found themselves on. When Eumenes rejected a proposal to join forces with Craterus (someone he regarded as a friend) and Antipater (an enemy), Craterus was then put in the position of having to attack Eumenes' troops at the **Battle of the Hellespont**. Craterus didn't expect much resistance, but sometimes things just don't go the way you plan.

(The main reason for their invasion, according to Plutarch, was to reduce the power of Perdiccas, and probably to keep him from making a reverse invasion into Europe. This is why, when Perdiccas was killed soon afterwards, Antipater saw little reason to continue his military activities in Asia.)

Vocabulary

commission: power

put himself in a posture of defense: Neoptolemus brought his troops to fight alongside those of Eumenes; but then they turned around and started fighting their "allies."

contrivance: skill in management

routed: beat, conquered

rallied: rounded up

vigilance: careful watching for signs of danger

sagacity: wisdom

peculiar address: unusual skill and dexterity

Minerva: the Greek goddess Athena

Ceres: Demeter, the Greek goddess of crops and fertility

of such moment: so important

in his own breast alone: to himself alone

retire: retreat

inveterate and mortal enemies: longstanding enemies who wished each other dead

galleys: ships powered mainly by banks of oars

the ham: the back part of the thigh, or thereabouts

mortal: fatal

inveterate: long-established

reviling: saying angry, abusive things

corslet: a piece of body armour

groin: the lower part of the body

People

Craterus: or Krateros; a top general under Alexander. He also happened to be the son-in-law of **Antipater**.

Ptolemy (#1): Ptolemy I Soter, an officer of Alexander who took over the Egyptian part of the empire

Alcetas: a Macedonian general; the brother of **Perdiccas**

Historic Occasions

321 B.C.: Battle of the Hellespont

Reading

Part One

But when **Craterus** and Antipater, having subdued the Greeks, advanced into Asia, **with intentions to quell the power of Perdiccas**, and were reported to design an invasion of Cappadocia, Perdiccas, resolving himself to march against **Ptolemy (#1)**, made Eumenes commander-in-chief of all the forces of Armenia and Cappadocia, and to that purpose wrote letters, requiring **Alcetas** and Neoptolemus to be obedient to Eumenes, and giving full **commission** to Eumenes to dispose and order all things as he thought fit. Alcetas flatly refused to serve, because his Macedonians, he said were ashamed to fight against Antipater, and loved Craterus so well, they were ready to receive him for their commander. Neoptolemus designed treachery against Eumenes, but was discovered; and being summoned, refused to obey, and **put himself in a posture of defense**.

Here Eumenes first found the benefit of his own foresight and **contrivance**, for his foot being beaten, he **routed** Neoptolemus with his horse, and took all his baggage; and coming up with his whole force upon the phalanx while broken and disordered in its flight, obliged the men to lay down their arms and take an oath to serve under him. Neoptolemus, with some few stragglers whom he **rallied**, fled to Craterus and Antipater.

Part Two

From them had come an embassy to Eumenes, inviting him over to their side, offering to secure him in his present government and to give him additional command, both of men and of territory, with the advantage of gaining his enemy Antipater to become his friend, and keeping Craterus his friend from turning to be his enemy. To which Eumenes replied that he could not so suddenly be reconciled to his old enemy Antipater, especially at a time when he saw him use his friends like enemies, but was ready to reconcile Craterus to Perdiccas, upon any and equitable terms; but in case of any aggression, he would resist the injustice to his last breath, and would rather lose his life than betray his word.

Antipater, receiving this answer, took time to consider upon the whole matter; when Neoptolemus arrived from his defeat and acquainted them with the ill success of his arms, and urged them to give him assistance, to come, both of them if possible, but Craterus at any rate; for the Macedonians loved him so excessively, that if they saw but his hat, or heard his voice, they would all pass over in a body with their arms. And in truth Craterus had a mighty name among them, and the soldiers after Alexander's death were extremely fond of him, remembering how he had often for their sakes incurred Alexander's displeasure, doing his best to withhold him when he (Alexander) began to follow the Persian fashions, and always maintaining the customs of his country, when, through pride and luxuriousness, they began to be disregarded. Craterus, therefore, sent on Antipater into Cilicia; and himself and Neoptolemus marched with a large division of the army against Eumenes; expecting to come upon him unawares, and to find his army disordered with revelling after the late victory.

Part Three

Now that Eumenes should suspect his coming, and be prepared to receive him, is an argument of his **vigilance**, but not perhaps a proof of any extraordinary **sagacity**; but that he should contrive both to conceal from his enemies the disadvantages of his position, and from his own men whom they were to fight with, so that he led them on against Craterus himself, without their knowing that he commanded the enemy: this, indeed, seems to show **peculiar address** and skill in the general. He gave out that Neoptolemus and Pigres were approaching with some Cappadocian and Paphlagonian horse.

And at night, having resolved on marching, he fell asleep, and had an extraordinary dream. For he thought he saw two Alexanders ready to engage, each commanding his several phalanx, the one assisted by **Minerva**, the other by **Ceres**; and that after a hot dispute, he on whose side Minerva was, was beaten, and Ceres, gathering ears of corn, wove them into a crown for the victor. This vision Eumenes interpreted at once as boding success to himself, who was to fight for a fruitful country, and at that very time covered with the young ears, the whole being sown with corn, and the fields so thick with it that they made a beautiful show of a long peace. And he was further emboldened when he understood that the enemy's password was "Minerva and Alexander." Accordingly he gave out as his password "Ceres and Alexander," and gave his men orders to make garlands for themselves, and to dress their arms with wreaths of corn. He found himself under many temptations to discover to his captains and officers whom they were to engage with, and not to conceal a secret **of such moment in his own breast alone**, yet he kept to his first resolutions, and ventured to run the hazard of his own judgment.

When he came to give battle, he would not trust any Macedonian to engage Craterus, but appointed two troops of foreign horse, commanded by Pharnabazus, son to Artabazus, and Phoenix of Tenedos, with order to charge as soon as ever they saw the enemy, without giving them leisure to speak or **retire**, or receiving any herald or trumpet from them. For he was exceedingly afraid about his Macedonians, lest, if they found out Craterus to be there, they should go over to his side.

He himself, with three hundred of his best horse, led the right wing against Neoptolemus. When having passed a little hill they came in view, and were seen advancing with more than ordinary briskness, Craterus was amazed, and bitterly reproached Neoptolemus for deceiving him with hopes of the Macedonians' revolt; but he encouraged his men to do bravely, and forthwith charged.

Part Four

The first engagement was very fierce, and the spears being soon broken to pieces, they came to close fighting with their swords; and here Craterus did by no means dishonour Alexander, but slew many of his enemies and repulsed many assaults; but at last he received a wound in his side from a Thracian, and fell off his horse. Being down, many, not knowing him, went past him; but Gorgias, one of Eumenes' captains, knew him, and alighting from his horse kept guard over him as he lay badly wounded and slowly dying.

In the meantime Neoptolemus and Eumenes were engaged; who, being **inveterate and mortal enemies**, sought for one another, but missed for the two first courses, but in the third discovering one another, they drew their swords, and with loud shouts immediately charged. And their horses striking against one another like two **galleys**, they quitted their reins, and taking mutual hold pulled at one another's helmets, and at the armour from their shoulders. While they were thus struggling, their horses went from under them, and they fell together to the ground, there again still keeping their hold and wrestling. Neoptolemus was getting up first, but Eumenes wounded him in **the ham**, and got upon his feet before him. Neoptolemus supporting himself upon one knee, the other leg being disabled, and himself undermost, fought courageously, though his blows were not **mortal**, but receiving a stroke in the neck he fell and ceased to resist. Eumenes, transported with passion and his **inveterate** hatred to him, fell to **reviling** and stripping him, and perceived not that his sword was still in his hand. And with this he wounded Eumenes under the bottom of his **corslet** in the **groin**, but in truth more frightened than hurt him; his blow being faint for want of strength.

Having stript the dead body, ill as he was with the wounds he had received in his legs and arms, he took horse again, and hurried towards the left wing of his army, which he supposed to be still engaged. Hearing of the death of Craterus, he rode up to him, and finding there was yet some life in him, alighted from his horse and wept, and laying his right hand upon him, inveighed bitterly against Neoptolemus, and lamented both Craterus's misfortune and his own hard fate, that he should be necessitated to engage against an old friend and acquaintance, and either do or suffer so much mischief.

Narration and Discussion

The ordinary soldiers were happy to serve under Eumenes, but Alcetas and Neoptolemus objected to his being chosen as commander. What might have been some of their reasons?

Why did Eumenes refuse the offer that Craterus made?

How was the victory at the Battle of the Hellespont a bittersweet one?

Character cards to add: Craterus, Ptolemy I Soter (#1)

Lesson Three

Introduction

Eumenes faced a mixed reaction after his victory at the Hellespont. Who was this young(ish) upstart who was, more or less, responsible for the death of Craterus? (Neoptolemus does not seem to have been as much missed.) He was now the official enemy of Antipater (although he never did end up fighting him), and Antigonus (who gave Eumenes a bad defeat at the Battle of Orkynia).

Vocabulary

This victory: at the Battle of the Hellespont (see **Lesson Two**)

the former: the fight against Neoptolemus

valour: bravery, courage

mutiny: rebellion by those under one's command

overseers: those responsible for keeping track of things like that

laudable: praiseworthy

engage: that is, fight with Antipater's troops. If Eumenes had been able to win such a battle, he would have gained power over most of **Asia Minor**. Because he was unsure of his military chances, he also tried to gain the support of Alexander's sister Cleopatra, who had the loyalty of many of his soldiers.

umbrage: annoyance

proportionably…: to pay each one what he was due

bestow purple hats and cloaks: This act had great significance, as it was usually a king who gave out these items of clothing. Eumenes may have even said that he was acting by the orders of or on behalf of the Macedonian royal family.

petty: small, insignificant

gathered up the dead bodies: This had a deep religious and cultural significance, but others were surprised that Eumenes would take the time and risk his own safety to carry out these rituals.

decamped: left, went home

posture: location, situation

People

Menander: one of Alexander's generals

Historic Occasions

320 B.C.: Death of Perdiccas

320 B.C.: Antipater became regent of Alexander's empire

319 B.C.: Death of Antipater; Polyperchon became regent of the empire (instead of Cassander, which caused Cassander to ally himself with Antigonus, Lysimachus, and Ptolemy)

319 B.C.: Antigonus invaded Cappadocia

319 B.C.: Battle of Orkynia in Cappadocia (the first battle fought between Antigonus and Eumenes)

On the Map

Plains of Lydia: Lydia was a kingdom of Asia Minor which became a satrapy of the Persian Empire. Its capital city was **Sardis**.

Celaenae: the capital city of Antigonus's satrapy

Orkynia: or Orcynii; battle site in Cappadocia (central Turkey)

Reading

Part One

This victory Eumenes obtained about ten days after **the former**, and got great reputation alike for his conduct and his **valour** in achieving it. But, on the other hand, it created him great envy both among his own troops and his enemies that he, a stranger and a foreigner, should employ the forces and arms of Macedon to cut off the bravest and most approved man among them. Had the news of this defeat come timely enough to Perdiccas, he had doubtless been the greatest of all the Macedonians; but now, he being slain in a **mutiny** in Egypt, two days before the news arrived, [his] Macedonians in a rage decreed Eumenes' death, giving joint commission to Antigonus and Antipater to prosecute the war against him.

Passing by Mount Ida, where there was a royal establishment of horses, Eumenes took as many as he had occasion for, and sent an account of his doing so to the **overseers**; at which Antipater is said to have laughed, calling it truly **laudable** in Eumenes thus to hold himself prepared for giving in to them (or would it be taking from them?) strict account of all matters of administration.

Eumenes had designed to **engage** in the **plains of Lydia**, near **Sardis**, both because his chief strength lay in horse, and to let Cleopatra see how powerful he was. But at her particular request, for she was afraid to give any **umbrage** to Antipater, he marched into the upper Phrygia, and wintered in **Celaenae** *[omission]*.

[Another reason that Eumenes did not fight with Antipater at this or any future time was that Antipater, no longer concerned with Perdiccas, and having more pressing interests back in Macedon, was soon headed for home; and he died there a few months later. His death is mentioned briefly in the next lesson.]

Part Two

Having promised his soldiers pay within three days, he sold them all the farms and castles in the country, together with the men and beasts with which they were filled; every captain or officer that bought [one of them] received from Eumenes the use of his engines to storm the place, and divided the spoils among his company, **proportionably to every man's arrears**.

By this Eumenes came again to be popular, so that when letters were found thrown about the camp by the enemy promising one hundred talents, besides great honours, to any one that should kill Eumenes, the Macedonians were extremely offended, and made an order that from that time forward one thousand of their best men should continually guard his person, and keep strict watch about him by night in their several turns. This order was cheerfully obeyed, and they gladly received of Eumenes the same honours which the kings used to confer upon their favourites. He now had leave to **bestow purple hats and cloaks**, which among the Macedonians is one of the greatest honours the king can give.

Good fortune will elevate even **petty** minds, and give them the appearance of a certain greatness and stateliness, as from their high place they look down upon the world; but the truly noble and resolved spirit raises itself, and becomes more conspicuous in times of disaster and ill fortune, as was now the case with Eumenes. For having by the treason of one of his own men lost the field to Antigonus at **Orkynia**, in Cappadocia, in his flight he gave the traitor no opportunity to escape to the enemy, but immediately seized and hanged him.

Then in his flight, taking a contrary course to his pursuers, he stole by them unawares, returned to the place where the battle had been fought, and encamped. There he **gathered up the dead bodies** and burnt them with the doors and windows of the neighbouring villages, and raised heaps of earth upon their graves; insomuch that Antigonus, who came thither soon after, expressed his astonishment at his courage and firm resolution.

Falling afterwards upon the baggage of Antigonus, he might easily have taken many captives, both bond and freemen, and much wealth collected from the spoils of so many wars; but he feared lest his men, overladen with so much booty, might become unfit for rapid retreat, and too fond of their ease to sustain the continual marches and endure the long waiting on which he depended for success, expecting to tire Antigonus into some other course. But then considering it would be extremely difficult to restrain the Macedonians from plunder, when it seemed to offer itself, he gave them order to refresh themselves, and bait their horses, and then attack the enemy. In the meantime he sent privately to **Menander**, who had care of all this baggage, professing a concern for him upon the score of old friendship and acquaintance; and therefore advising him to quit the plain and secure himself upon the sides of the neighbouring hills, where the horse might not be able to hem him in. When Menander, sensible of his danger, had speedily packed up his goods and **decamped**, Eumenes openly sent his scouts to discover the enemy's **posture**, and commanded his men to arm and bridle their horses, as designing immediately to give battle; but the scouts returning with news that Menander had secured so difficult a post it was impossible to take him, Eumenes, pretending to be grieved with the disappointment, drew off his men another way *[omission for content]*.

Narration and Discussion

Eumenes' part in the death of Craterus angered many Macedonians. Why didn't his own men feel the same way (even when they were offered a reward to kill him)?

Why didn't Eumenes want his men to loot the enemy's camp? (Remember that the "baggage" would also include human "loot.")

What are some ways that Eumenes showed a "truly noble and resolved spirit" at this time?

For further thought or debate: "…the truly noble and resolved spirit raises itself, and becomes more conspicuous in times of disaster and ill fortune." Do you agree?

Creative narration: Write or act out a conversation between two soldiers who have received "purple hats."

Lesson Four

Introduction

Eumenes had escaped capture after the Battle of Orkynia, but he was now in the position of a fugitive. He persuaded some of his soldiers to go home, but shut himself with the remainder into a fort called Nora. Besieged there by Antigonus (and passing the time by creating a sort of treadmill to exercise the horses), he eventually managed to negotiate an end to the stalemate, though somewhat deceitfully. As a result, Eumenes became both a fugitive (again) and a sort of Superman character, getting letters requesting his help from everyone including the Queen Mother Olympias, who wanted him to protect Alexander's young son. Another letter, this one from the new regent Polyperchon, could not be ignored: he was ordered to fight again with Antigonus, on behalf of the "other" king (Alexander's half-brother). But at least he was promised all the material resources possible, plus the help of Alexander's famous Silver Shields.

Vocabulary

disband: leave the group, go home

confines: borders

license: permission

in his room: in his place

miscarry: fail

confirmed in his several governments: that he should be confirmed as the satrap of the two territories promised to him

restitution be made him of the rewards of his service: he should receive whatever money or other rewards he had been promised

beleaguered and kept garrison: surrounded by enemy forces; besieged

affable: friendly, good-natured

countenance: face

florid: having a red or flushed complexion

orator: one who is skillful at public speaking

two furlongs in compass: a quarter mile around (about 400 m)

curvet: a prancing leap

embroiled: involved in conflict

the differences of Cassander and Polyperchon: they were struggling for control of Alexander's empire

upon which he conceived no mean hopes: which gave him an idea that he could use this as his own opportunity to win power

letters from Polyperchon: These are significant because they show that the new regent Polyperchon, worried by the alliance that Cassander had made with Antigonus, saw Eumenes as his last, best hope of survival.

emulation: in this context, jealousy

regal pavilion: royal tent

prevailed upon: persuaded

affairs of moment: important matters

decease: death

imperious: arrogant

pampered in their conceit: encouraged to continue in their inflated ideas

dissolute: immoral, sinful

canvassed: To canvass is to go around from person to person or house to house to gather support for a cause, for instance before an election.

severally: separately, in various places

People

Ptolemy (#2): or Ptolemaeus; Macedonian general who was nephew to Antigonus

Polyperchon: sometimes spelled Polysperchon; a Macedonian general chosen by Antipater to be his successor as regent of the empire, a choice which caused great conflict between those loyal to either Polyperchon or Cassander.

Antigenes: a Macedonian general who was satrap of **Susiana** (a territory also called **Elam**); one of the commanders of the Silver Shields, who were in Cilicia at this time

Teutamus: the other commander of the Silver Shields

Peucestas: or Peucestes; an officer in Alexander's army, and the satrap (governor) of Persis. After the death of Alexander, he continued as satrap, and wanted to extend his power even further; he has been called "vain and ambitious." In this war, he hoped to be the chief commander, and was not very pleased when the command was given to Eumenes, but he did stay loyal during the battles that followed. Unfortunately, he also seems to have been to blame for his side's defeat by Antigonus at the Battle of Gabiene.

Historic Occasions

317 B.C.: Battle of the Coprates River

On the Map

Nora: a fortress between Cappadocia and Lycaonia

Cyinda: or Quinda, or Kundi; a fortress city in Anatolia which was used to store treasure

into the interior of Asia: apparently Syria and Phoenicia

Susa: (not specifically named here): an important city in the former Persian Empire. It was near Susa that Eumenes met with the satraps, including Peucestas.

Reading

Part One

From this time Eumenes, daily flying and wandering about, persuaded many of his men to **disband**, whether out of kindness to them, or unwillingness to lead about such a body of men as were too few to engage and too many to fly undiscovered. Taking refuge at **Nora**, a place on the **confines** of Lycaonia and Cappadocia, with five hundred horse and two hundred heavy-armed foot, he again dismissed as many of his friends as desired it, through fear of the probable hardships to be encountered there, and embracing them with all demonstrations of kindness gave them **license** to depart.

Antigonus, when he came before this fort, desired to have an interview with Eumenes before the siege; but he returned answer that Antigonus had many friends who might command **in his room**; but they whom Eumenes defended had nobody to substitute if he should **miscarry**; therefore, if Antigonus thought it worthwhile to treat with him, he should first send him hostages. And when Antigonus required that Eumenes should first address himself to him as his superior, he replied, "While I am able to wield a sword, I shall think no man greater than myself."

At last, when, according to Eumenes's demand, Antigonus sent his own nephew **Ptolemy (#2)** to the fort, Eumenes went out to him (Antigonus), and they mutually embraced with great tenderness and friendship *[omission]*. After long conversation, Eumenes making no mention of his own pardon and security, but requiring that he should be **confirmed in his several governments**, and **restitution be made him of the rewards of his service**, all that were present were astonished at his courage and gallantry. And many of the Macedonians flocked to see what sort of person Eumenes was, for since the death of Craterus no man had been so much talked of in the army. But Antigonus, being afraid lest he might suffer some violence, first commanded the soldiers to keep off, calling out and throwing stones at those who pressed forwards. At last, taking Eumenes in his arms, and keeping off the crowd with his guards, not without great difficulty, he returned him safe into the fort.

Then Antigonus, having built a wall round Nora, left a force sufficient to carry on the siege, and drew off the rest of his army; and Eumenes was **beleaguered and kept garrison**, having plenty of corn and water and salt, but no other thing, either for food or delicacy; yet with such as he had, he kept a cheerful table for his friends, inviting them severally in their turns, and seasoning his entertainment with a gentle and **affable** behaviour. For he had a pleasant **countenance**, and looked not like an old and practised soldier, but was smooth and **florid**, and his shape as delicate as if his limbs had been carved by art in the most accurate proportions. He was not a great **orator**, but winning and persuasive, as may be seen in his letters.

The greatest distress of the besieged was the narrowness of the place they were in, their quarters being very confined, and the whole place but **two furlongs in compass**; so that both they and their horses fed without exercise. Accordingly, not only to prevent the listlessness of such inactive living, but to have them in condition to fly if occasion required, he assigned a room one-and-twenty feet long, the largest in all the fort, for the men to walk in, directing them to begin their walk gently, and so gradually mend their pace. And for the horses, he tied them to the roof with great halters, fastening which about their necks, with a pulley he gently raised them, till standing upon the ground with their hinder feet, they just touched it with the very ends of their forefeet. In this posture the grooms plied them with whips and shouts, provoking them to **curvet** and kick out with their hind legs, struggling and stamping at the same time to find support for their forefeet, and thus their whole body was exercised, till they were all in a foam and sweat; excellent exercise, whether for strength or speed;

and then he gave them their corn already coarsely ground, that they might sooner despatch and better digest it.

The siege continuing long, Antigonus received advice that Antipater was dead in Macedon, and that affairs were **embroiled** by **the differences of Cassander and Polyperchon; upon which he conceived no mean hopes**, purposing to make himself master of all.

[Omission for length: Antigonus sent messengers to Eumenes, offering to make him his second-in-command. He proposed an oath of loyalty, but Eumenes disagreed with the wording and sent back a revised version, in which he swore loyalty to the two Macedonian kings, but not to Antigonus himself. The siege was lifted, but Eumenes was now in trouble, so he gathered his horsemen and fled.]

Part Two

While Eumenes was flying, he received letters from those in Macedonia who were jealous of Antigonus's greatness: from Olympias, inviting him thither to take the charge and protection of Alexander's infant son, whose person was in danger; and other **letters from Polyperchon** and Philip the king, requiring him to make war upon Antigonus, as general of the forces in Cappadocia; and empowering him out of the treasure at **Cynda** to take five hundred talents as compensation for his own losses, and to levy as much as he thought necessary to carry on the war. They wrote also to the same effect to **Antigenes** and **Teutamus**, the chief officers of the Silver Shields; who, on receiving these letters, treated Eumenes with a show of respect and kindness; but it was apparent enough that they were full of envy and **emulation**, disdaining to give place to him. Their envy Eumenes moderated by refusing to accept the money, as if he had not needed it; and their ambition and emulation, who were neither able to govern nor willing to obey, he conquered by help of superstition. For he told them that Alexander had appeared to him in a dream, and showed him a **regal pavilion** richly furnished, with a throne in it; and told him if they would sit in council there, he himself (Alexander) would be present, and prosper all the consultations and actions upon which they should enter in his name.

Antigenes and Teutamus were easily **prevailed upon** to believe this, being as little willing to come and consult Eumenes as he himself was to be seen waiting at other men's doors. Accordingly, they erected a tent royal, and a throne, called "Alexander's," and there they met to consult upon all **affairs of moment**.

Part Three

Afterwards they advanced **into the interior of Asia**, and in their march met with **Peucestas**, who was friendly to them, and with the other satraps, who joined forces with them, and greatly encouraged the Macedonians with the number and appearance of their men. But they themselves, having since Alexander's **decease** become **imperious** and ungoverned in their tempers, and luxurious in their daily habits, imagining themselves great princes, and **pampered in their conceit** by the flattery of the barbarians, when all these conflicting pretensions now came together, were soon found to be exacting and quarrelsome one with another, while all alike unmeasurably flattered the Macedonians, giving them money for revels and sacrifices, till in a short time they brought the camp to be a **dissolute** place of entertainment, and the army a mere multitude of voters, **canvassed** as in a democracy for the election of this or that commander. Eumenes, perceiving they despised one another, and all of them feared him, and sought an opportunity to kill him, pretended to be in want of money, and borrowed many talents, of those especially who most hated him, to make them at once confide in him and forbear all violence to him for fear of losing their own money. Thus his enemies' estates were the guard of his person, and by receiving money he purchased safety, for which it is more common to give it.

The Macedonians, also, while there was no show of danger, allowed themselves to be corrupted, and made all their court to those who gave them presents, who had their body-guards, and affected to appear generals-in-chief. But when Antigonus came upon them with a great army, and their affairs themselves seemed to call out for a true general, then not only the common soldiers cast their eyes upon Eumenes, but these men, who had appeared so great in a peaceful time of ease, submitted all of them to him, and quietly posted themselves **severally** as he appointed them.

[Omission for length and addition for clarity: the Battle of the Coprates River,

which is given only a short mention by Plutarch. Eumenes took 4,000 of Antigonus's men prisoner, and seemed to be the clear winner. Having control of the river meant that Antigonus's remaining troops could not cross it, and therefore had to head north, into the Zagros Mountains. It seemed that Eumenes had carried out his mission by defeating Antigonus, and he intended to move his troops westward, towards the Mediterranean sea. However, that did not please some of his Eastern allies, because that would mean leaving their territories unguarded. Eumenes agreed to follow their lead, and they all moved east, to the city of Persepolis. What they didn't realize was that Antigonus's troops had circled the mountains, and were now headed back in their direction.]

Narration and Discussion

How did Eumenes persuade the satraps, first of all, not to kill him, and second, to choose him as their commander-in-chief?

"While I am able to wield a sword, I shall think no man greater than myself." Is this a good philosophy of life? How would you respond to Eumenes?

For older students: What was Eumenes' unusual way of using the power of money? Is that something you would ever try doing in real life? (For Christian students: The book of Proverbs has a few equally interesting suggestions that Eumenes might have appreciated, such as Prov. 17:8, 21:14.)

Character cards to add: Polyperchon; Olympias (optional); Peucestas; Cassander; The Silver Shields, or Antigenes and Teutamus.

Lesson Five

Introduction

We begin this lesson with a story about how Eumenes, at some point in this campaign, stayed in command even from his sickbed. For some in his camp, that made him worthy of great praise; but others seemed to resent or not trust him as their leader. The events that came next were very important: first, the Battle of Paraetacene, although Plutarch does not include much about that; and then the final Battle of Gabiene.

Vocabulary

having been dangerously ill: Plutarch never explains what was wrong with Eumenes; in any case, he seems to have recovered afterwards.

in a litter: on a bed that could be carried

castles on their backs: also called howdahs or houdahs; carriages set on the backs of elephants

pikes: long spears

withdrew his forces: Plutarch credits Eumenes' performance here as the cause of Antigonus's retreat; but the historian Diodorus says that it was more a case of neither side liking the terrain very much, and deciding to wait for another time and place to fight.

checked: stopped

dromedaries: camels with one hump

expresses: speedy messengers

muster: gather, collect

an elevated tract: a raised piece of ground

vexation: annoyance

despondency: gloominess, sadness

skirmishes: minor battles

stratagem: trick, scheme

commended: praised

expedients: possibilities

versatile: adaptable, flexible

Historic Occasions

317 B.C.: Battle of Paraetacene (or Paraitakene), the second battle between Antigonus and Eumenes

316 B.C.: Battle of Gabiene, the third battle between Antigonus and Eumenes; the end of the Second War of the Diadochi

On the Map

Gabenes, Gabiene, Gabeni: A plain on the Iranian Plateau, in the middle of what was then Persia; the site of Eumenes' final battle. There are various spellings for this place; for consistency, we will refer to it as the **Battle of Gabiene**.

Media: a region now part of northwestern Iran

Reading

Part One

But it was most particularly when Eumenes was sick that the Macedonians let it be seen how in their judgment, while others could feast them handsomely and make entertainments, he alone knew how to fight and lead an army. For Peucestas, having made a splendid entertainment in Persia, and given each of the soldiers a sheep to sacrifice with, made himself sure of being commander-in-chief.

Some few days after the army was to march, and Eumenes **having been dangerously ill** was carried **in a litter** apart from the body of the army, that any rest he got might not be disturbed. But when they were a little advanced, unexpectedly they had a view of the enemy, who had passed the hills that lay between them, and was marching down into the plain. At the sight of the golden armour glittering in the sun as they marched down in their order, the elephants with their **castles on their backs**, and the men in their purple, as their manner was when they were going to give battle, the front stopped their march, and called out for Eumenes, for they would not advance a step but under his conduct; and fixing their arms in the ground gave the word among themselves to stand, requiring their officers also not to stir or engage or hazard themselves without Eumenes. News of this being brought to Eumenes, he hastened those that carried his litter, and drawing back the curtains on both sides, joyfully put forth his right hand. As soon as the soldiers saw him they saluted him in their Macedonian dialect, and took up their shields, and striking them with their **pikes**, gave a great shout; inviting the enemy to come on, for now they had a leader.

Antigonus understanding by some prisoners he had taken that Eumenes was out of health, to that degree that he was carried in a litter, presumed it would be no hard matter to crush the rest of them, since he was ill. He therefore made the greater haste to come up with them and engage. But being come so near as to discover how the enemy was drawn up and appointed, he was astonished, and paused for some time; at last he saw the litter carrying from one wing of the army to the other, and, as his manner was, laughing aloud, he said to his friends, "That litter there, it seems, is the thing that offers us battle;" and immediately wheeled about and [**withdrew his forces**].

*[The second battle between Antigonus and Eumenes was the **Battle of Paraetacene**, again fought in 317 B.C. In Plutarch's narrative, it is a bit hard to distinguish this from the other events, especially as he focuses his story on the incident involving Eumenes' illness, which took place at some point while the armies were on the march. In any case, this second battle was a formal, well-planned one, making use of cavalry, infantry, and even elephants (on both sides). Both sides claimed the victory, but Eumenes' side lost only about 500 men, compared to almost 4,000 for Antigonus. At this point Antigonus returned to **Media**, and Eumenes marched his troops east. The expectation was that fighting would not resume until after the winter; but Antigonus planned a surprise.]*

Part Two

[Eumenes' troops took up winter quarters in the Gabiene region], so that the front was quartered nearly a thousand furlongs from the rear; which Antigonus understanding, marched suddenly towards them, taking the most difficult road through a country that wanted water; but the way was short though uneven; hoping, if he should surprise them thus scattered in their winter quarters, the soldiers would not easily be able to come up in time enough and join with their officers. But having to pass through a country uninhabited, where he met with violent winds and severe frosts, he was much **checked** in his march, and his men suffered exceedingly. The only possible relief was making numerous fires, by which his enemies got notice of his coming.

For the barbarians who dwelt on the mountains overlooking the desert, amazed at the multitude of fires they saw, sent messengers upon **dromedaries** to acquaint Peucestas. He being astonished and almost out of his senses with the news, and finding the rest in no less disorder, resolved to fly, and collect what men he could by the way. But Eumenes relieved him from his fear and trouble, undertaking so to stop the enemy's advance that he should arrive three days later than he was expected.

Having persuaded them, he immediately despatched **expresses** to all the officers to draw the men out of their winter quarters and **muster** them with all speed. He himself, with some of the chief officers, rode out, and chose **an elevated tract** within view, at a distance, of such as travelled the desert; this he occupied and quartered out, and commanded many fires to be made in it, as the custom is in a camp.

This done, and the enemies seeing the fire upon the mountains, Antigonus was filled with **vexation** and **despondency**, supposing that his enemies had been long since advertised of his march, and were prepared to receive him. Therefore, lest his army, now tired and wearied out with their march, should be immediately forced to encounter with fresh men, who had wintered well and were ready for him, quitting the near way, he marched slowly through the towns and villages to refresh his men.

But meeting with no such **skirmishes** as are usual when two armies lie near one another, and being assured by the people of the country that no army had been seen, but only continual fires at that place, he concluded he had been outwitted by a **stratagem** of Eumenes, and, much troubled, advanced to give open battle.

Interlude: Nasty Plans

By this time, the greater part of the forces were come together to Eumenes, and admiring his sagacity, declared him alone commander-in-chief of the whole army; upon which Antigenes and Teutamus, the commanders of the Silver Shields, being very much offended, and envying Eumenes, formed a conspiracy against him; and assembling the greater part of the satraps and officers, consulted when and how to cut him off. When they had unanimously agreed, first to use his service in the next battle, and then to take an occasion to destroy him, Eudamus, the master of the elephants, and Phaedimus gave Eumenes private advice of this design, not out of kindness or good-will to him, but lest they should lose the money they had lent him.

Eumenes, having **commended** them, retired to his tent, and telling his friends he lived among a herd of wild beasts, made his will, and tore up all his letters, lest his correspondents after his death should be questioned or punished on account of anything in his secret papers.

Part Three

Having thus disposed of his affairs, he thought of letting the enemy win the field; or of flying through **Media** and Armenia and seizing Cappadocia; but came to no resolution while his friends stayed with him. After turning to many **expedients** in his mind, which his changeable fortune had made **versatile**, he at last put his men in array, and encouraged the Greeks and barbarians; as for the phalanx and the Silver Shields, they encouraged him, and bade him be of good heart, for the enemy would never be able to stand them. For indeed they were the oldest of Philip's and Alexander's soldiers, tried men, that had long made war their exercise, that had never been beaten or foiled; most of them seventy, none less than sixty years old.

And so when they charged Antigonus's men, they cried out, "You fight against your fathers, you rascals," and furiously falling on them, routed the whole phalanx at once, nobody being able to stand them, and the greatest part dying by their hands.

[Plutarch gives few details about how the Battle of Gabiene was fought, but perhaps none are really needed after that final paragraph.]

Narration and Discussion

Choose four to six events that you believe are important here, and write them down the left-hand side of a piece of paper. On the right-hand side, write down (if you can) who was involved, what caused it, and what it did (or could) lead to. If you are working with a group, compare your answers with those of others.

Creative narration: Retell the story from the point of view of Antigonus.

Lesson Six

Introduction

Eumenes was betrayed by the Silver Shields (who now thought of him as a "Chersonesian pest"), and handed over to his somewhat reluctant captor. What should be done, Antigonus wondered, with a former friend who might easily have had him in the same position?

Vocabulary

> **became master of the baggage:** was able to capture everything belonging to the Silver Shields
>
> **behaved himself negligently and basely:** Peucestes panicked when things were not going well, causing a large number of horsemen to withdraw from the battle.
>
> **girdle:** belt, sash
>
> **deprecate:** express disapproval of; speak against
>
> **redeem your stuff:** This sounds impossibly modern, but "stuff" has long been used to mean material goods.
>
> **perjury:** dishonesty (especially under oath)
>
> **trifling:** speaking of trivial things; messing around
>
> **defrauded of the fruits of so long service:** cheated of the treasure they had gathered over so many years (not to mention having their family members taken captive)
>
> **lances:** soldiers with spears

press: crowd, mob

importunate: persistent

despatch: kill

contumeliously: in a scornful and insulting way

taken off: killed

Divine Providence: A term usually referring to Almighty God; other translations refer more generally to Greek gods.

chastisement: rebuke, punishment

abominating: despising

People

Nicanor: a general who supported Cassander

Historic Occasions

316 B.C.: Capture and death of Eumenes

On the Map

Arachosia: a region which is now part of southern Afghanistan

Reading

Part One

So that Antigonus's foot was routed, but his horse got the better, and he **became master of the baggage** through the cowardice of Peucestas, who **behaved himself negligently and basely**; while Antigonus used his judgment calmly in the danger, being aided moreover by the ground. For the place where they fought was a large plain, neither deep nor hard under foot, but, like the seashore, covered with a fine soft sand which the treading of so many men and horses in the time of battle reduced to a small white dust, that like a cloud of lime darkened the air, so that one could not see clearly at any distance, and so made it easy for Antigonus's men to take the baggage unperceived.

[The battle seemed to be done for the day, and Eumenes expected to wind things up with a final victory over Antigonus. However, as the two sides were retreating to their camps for the night, the news came that the Silver Shields' baggage train had been captured.]

Teutamus sent a message to Antigonus to demand the baggage. He made answer, he would not only restore it to the Silver Shields, but serve them further in the other things if they would but deliver up Eumenes. Upon which the Silver Shields took a villainous resolution to deliver him up alive into the hands of his enemies.

Part Two

So they came to wait upon him, being unsuspected by him, but watching their opportunity, some lamenting the loss of the baggage, some encouraging him as if he had been victor, some accusing the other commanders, till at last they all fell upon him, and seizing his sword, bound his hands behind him with his own **girdle**.

When Antigonus had sent **Nicanor** to receive him, he begged he might be led through the body of the Macedonians, and have liberty to speak to them, neither to request nor **deprecate** anything, but only to advise them what would be for their interest.

A silence being made, as he stood upon a rising ground, he stretched out his hands bound, and said,

> "What trophy, O ye basest of all the Macedonians,
> could Antigonus have wished for so great as you
> yourselves have erected for him in delivering up
> your general captive into his hands? You are not
> ashamed, when you are conquerors, to own
> yourselves conquered, for the sake only of your
> baggage, as if it were wealth, not arms, wherein
> victory consisted; nay, you deliver up your
> general to **redeem your stuff**. As for me I am

92

unvanquished, though a captive, conqueror of my
enemies, and betrayed by my fellow-soldiers. For
you, I adjure you by Jupiter, the protector of arms,
and by all the gods that are the avengers of
perjury, to kill me here with your own hands; for it
is all one; and if I am murdered yonder it will be
esteemed your act, nor will Antigonus complain, for
he desires not Eumenes alive, but dead. Or if you
withhold your own hands, release but one of mine,
it shall suffice to do the work; and if you dare not
trust me with a sword, throw me bound as I am
under the feet of the wild beasts. This if you do I
shall freely acquit you from the guilt of my death, as
the most just and kind of men to their general."

While Eumenes was thus speaking, the rest of the soldiers wept for
grief; but the Silver Shields shouted out to lead him on, and give
no attention to his **trifling**. For it was no such great matter if this
Chersonesian pest should meet his death, who in thousands of battles
had annoyed and wasted the Macedonians; it would be a much more
grievous thing for the choicest of Philip's and Alexander's soldiers to
be **defrauded of the fruits of so long service**, and in their old age to
come to beg their bread, and to leave their wives three nights in the
power of their enemies. So they hurried him on with violence.

Part Three

But Antigonus, fearing the multitude, for nobody was left in the camp,
sent ten of his strongest elephants with [numerous] Mede and Parthian
lances to **keep off the press**. Then he could not endure to have
Eumenes brought into his presence, by reason of their former intimacy
and friendship; but when they that had taken him inquired how he
would have him kept: "As I would," said he, "an elephant, or a lion."

A little after, being moved with compassion, he commanded the
heaviest of Eumenes' irons to be knocked off, one of his servants to
be admitted to anoint him, and that any of his friends that were willing
should have liberty to visit him, and bring him what he wanted. Long
time he deliberated what to do with him, sometimes inclining to the
advice and promises of Nearchus of Crete, and Demetrius his son,

who were very earnest to preserve Eumenes; whilst all the rest were unanimously instant and **importunate** to have him **taken off**. It is related that Eumenes inquired of Onomarchus, his keeper, why Antigonus, now he had his enemy in his hands, would not forthwith **despatch** or generously release him? And that Onomarchus **contumeliously** answered him, that the field had been a more proper place than this to show his contempt of death.

To whom Eumenes replied, "And, by heavens, I showed it there; ask the men else that engaged me, but I could never meet a man that was my superior."

"Therefore," rejoined Onomarchus, "now you have found such a man, why don't you submit quietly to his pleasure?"

Part Four

When Antigonus resolved to kill Eumenes, he commanded to keep his food from him, and so with two or three days' fasting he began to draw near his end; but the camp being on a sudden to remove, an executioner was sent to despatch him.

Antigonus granted his body to his friends, permitted them to burn it, and having gathered his ashes into a silver urn, to send them to his wife and children. Eumenes was thus taken off, and **Divine Providence** assigned to no other man the **chastisement** of the commanders and soldiers that had betrayed him; but Antigonus himself, **abominating** the Silver Shields as wicked and inhuman villains, delivered them up to Sibyrtius, the governor of **Arachosia**, commanding him by all ways and means to destroy and exterminate them, so that not a man of them might ever come to Macedon, or so much as within sight of the Greek Sea.

Narration and Discussion

Should Eumenes have expected his betrayal? Were there clues that he ignored?

In C.S. Lewis's Narnia book *The Last Battle*, there is a war between those who believe in Aslan and those who support Tash. The dwarfs, however, say that "the dwarfs are for the dwarfs." Can you see any parallels to the events of this lesson?

Character cards to add: Nicanor; Demetrius. As a review, choose one of your character cards and tell as much as you can about the person or persons represented. For a greater challenge, ask someone else to choose a card for you to narrate.

Creative narration: You are the editor of the Macedonian Daily News (you can choose a better name), and you have just received the shocking news of Eumenes' death. You will need to quickly pull your files together and write a front-page story about him for the newspaper. What will you include? Who might you talk to?

Examination Questions

For younger students:

1. What part did the Silver Shields play in a) Eumenes' success, and b) his death? (Or use the first question suggested for older students.)

2. If you have made *Diadochi* Character Cards, choose one card and tell as much as you can about the person represented.

For older students:

1. Eumenes showed deep loyalty to his (adopted) Macedonian rulers. Give two examples. (Or use the questions suggested for younger students.)

2. (High school) Eumenes often found himself in situations where his right to lead was questioned. Give examples, and tell how he dealt with each situation. For example, how did he win the confidence of the eastern satraps?

   Alternative Question: Plutarch wrote of the time right after Alexander's death, "when the quarrel broke out between the troops of the phalanx and the officers, [Alexander's] companions; [but] Eumenes, though in his judgment he inclined to the latter, yet in his professions stood neuter, as if he thought it unbecoming him, who was a stranger, to interpose in the private quarrels of the Macedonians." Why does this statement seem ironic?

Appendix D: The PNEU Plutarch Program

Which of Plutarch's *Lives* were covered in the PNEU School programmes, and which ones were skipped (for whatever reason)? The early programmes (from the 1890's) tended to be vague about what was to be covered: a typical one simply suggests "Greek History: Twelve narrations from Plutarch's *Lives*."

Owls and Dragons

Somewhat later programmes (ca. 1905) suggest a particular life for each term, using the Cassell's National Library edition, but without any other reference materials; the Cassell's edition uses the Langhorne translation rather than North's. I noticed something interesting about the Langhorne version: there are lots of helpful footnotes, which may have stood in for the extra resources used later on.

Here's a passage from Langhorne's *Life of Demosthenes*, and then the same passage from North's and Dryden's for comparison.

> It is said, that when he was not far from the city, he perceived some of his late adversaries following, and endeavoured to hide himself. But they called to him by name; and when they came nearer, desired him to take some necessary supplies of money, which they had brought with them for that purpose: They assured him, they had no other design in following; and exhorted him to take courage. But Demosthenes gave into more violent expressions of grief than ever, and said, "What comfort can I have, when I leave enemies in this city more generous than it seems, possible to find friends in any other?"... When he left Athens, we are told, he lifted up his hands towards the citadel, and said, "O Minerva, goddess of those towers, whence is it that thou delightest in three such monsters as an owl, a dragon, and the people?"

The same passage from North:

Some do report that he fled not far from the city :
where it was told him that certain of his enemies
followed him, whereupon he would have hidden
himself from them. But they themselves first called
him by his name, and coming to him, prayed him to
take money of them, which they had brought him
from their houses to help him in his banishment :
and that therefore they ran after him. Then they did
comfort him the best they could, and persuaded
him to be of good cheer, and not to despair for the
misfortune that was come unto him. This did pierce
his heart the more for sorrow, that he answered
them : Why, would you not have me be sorry for my
misfortune, that compelleth me to forsake the city
where indeed I have so courteous enemies, that it is
hard for me to find anywhere so good friends ?...
For it is reported of him, that as he went out of
Athens, he looked back again, and holding up his
hands to the castle, said in this sort: O Lady
Minerva, lady patroness of this city : why doest thou
delight in three so mischievous beasts : the owl, the
dragon, and the people?

Dryden:

We are told, at least, that he had not fled far from
the city when, finding that he was pursued by some
of those who had been his adversaries, he
endeavoured to hide himself. But when they called
him by his name, and coming up nearer to him,
desired he would accept from them some money
which they had brought from home as a provision
for his journey, and to that purpose only
had followed him, when they entreated him to take
courage, and to bear up against his misfortune, he
burst out into much greater lamentation, saying,
"But how is it possible to support myself under so
heavy an affliction, since I leave a city in which I
have such enemies, as in any other it is not easy to
find friends." ... For, as he was departing out of the
city, it is reported, he lifted up his hands towards

Appendix D

Prog. 118: Themistocles (Blackie)

Prog. 119: Nicias (Blackie)

Prog. 120: Solon (Blackie)

Which *Lives* were not covered during this ten-year period?

Theseus	Crassus
Romulus	Sertorius
Lycurgus	Eumenes
Numa Pompilius	Agesilaus
Poplicola/Publicola	Phocion
Camillus	Cato the Younger
Fabius	Cicero
Pelopidas	Demetrius
Marcellus	Antony
Philopoemen	Dion
Caius/Gaius Marius	Aratus
Lysander	Artaxerxes
Sylla/Sulla	Galba
Cimon	Otho
Lucullus	

We cannot assume, however, that none of these were ever included in the curriculum. In the early years of the PNEU, a wider variety of *Lives* might have been used from standard editions. In Charlotte Mason's 1905 book *Ourselves*, for example, quotes are included from Plutarch's *Alexander*, *Lycurgus*, *Alcibiades*, and *Phocion*, implying that students would be familiar with them. Her last book, *Philosophy of Education*, includes a quote from a teacher who said "They cannot have enough of *Publicola*"; yet it hadn't been assigned for at least a couple of years.

In the period right after Charlotte Mason's death (in 1923), there seems to have been a short experiment using standard translations of Plutarch; but this did not last long, and the programmes soon went back to the limited number of *Lives* available through the Cambridge and Blackie student editions. This may mean that teachers, including parents or governesses, were less familiar with Plutarch and/or ancient history, and wanted to be on safer ground than simply being told to "make necessary omissions." Or perhaps they were moving away from the days when only the teacher had a copy of an expensive book, and they wanted something affordable and accessible for the students.

If someone someday uncovers a treasure trove of 1906-1920 PNEU programmes, we may get more satisfactory answers to these questions.

Appendix E: The AmblesideOnline Plutarch Program

(Included with the permission of AmblesideOnline)

The AmblesideOnline Curriculum has a ten-year cycle for Plutarch's *Lives* (without repeats). The *Life of Publicola* is not in the regular rotation, but is suggested as a first study; another suggestion for beginners is to do a children's-Plutarch version of the *Life of Theseus*. Students who are still not quite ready for Plutarch may follow the PNEU tradition of spending a year on *Stories from the History of Rome* by Emily Beesly. Teachers/students do not have to follow the cycle but are free to start at the beginning, or to choose particular studies which suit their needs. Some go more slowly and do only one or two per year.

The AO cycle has drawn, for the most part, on those *Lives* that were included in the PNEU programmes. Year 10 was envisioned as a slightly different and more challenging set of studies, though not beyond the capabilities of most students.

Year One
Term 1: Marcus Cato the Censor
Term 2: Philopoemen
Term 3: Titus Flamininus

Year Two
Term 1: Pyrrhus
Term 2: Nicias
Term 3: Crassus

Year Three
Term 1: Julius Caesar
Term 2: Agis and Cleomenes
Term 3: Tiberius Gracchus and Gaius Gracchus

Year Four
Term 1: Demosthenes

Term 2: Cicero
Term 3: Demetrius

Year Five
Term 1: Alexander, Part 1
Term 2: Alexander, Part 2
Term 3: Timoleon

Year Six
Term 1: Aemilius Paulus
Term 2: Aristides
Term 3: Solon

Year Seven
Term 1: Pompey, Part 1
Term 2: Pompey, Part 2
Term 3: Themistocles

Year Eight
Term 1: Marcus Brutus
Term 2: Pericles
Term 3: Fabius

Year Nine
Term 1: Alcibiades
Term 2: Coriolanus
Term 3: Cato the Younger

Year Ten
Term 1: Phocion
Term 2: Camillus
Term 3: Dion

Non-Plutarchian Glossary

AmblesideOnline: A free, online Charlotte Mason-based homeschool curriculum. www.amblesideonline.org

Charlotte Mason Digital Collection: A database containing documents and manuscripts relating to the work of Charlotte Mason and the PNEU.
https://www.redeemer.ca/academics/library/charlotte-mason-digital-collection/

"Education is an atmosphere, a discipline, and a life": the PNEU motto.

Form: A method of dividing school grade levels which was used by the PNEU. Form I corresponded to what North Americans call the primary grades; Form II would be the junior grades; Form III would be middle school; Form IV was approximately ninth grade; and Forms V and VI were senior high school. The study of Plutarch's *Lives* was begun in the second year of Form II (at about the age of ten), and continued through Form IV.

l'HaRMaS: An annual retreat for Charlotte Mason educators, held in Kingsville, Ontario, Canada.
https://www.prov-en-der.com/l-harmas.html

Parents' Review: The monthly magazine of the PNEU, originally edited by Charlotte Mason.

PNEU: Parents' National Education[al] Union; the organization headed by Charlotte Mason during her lifetime (and continued by others afterwards). The PNEU offered correspondence lessons for students in England and overseas, and there were (and are) also some bricks-and-mortar PNEU schools.

Programme: One term's work in all subjects, divided by forms.

Bibliography

Books

Bestvater, L. (2013). *The living page: Keeping notebooks with Charlotte Mason.* [Location not given]: Underpinnings Press.

Collins, M., & Tamarkin, C. (1990). *Marva Collins' way (2nd ed.).* Los Angeles, CA: J.P. Tarcher.

Karon, J. (2014). *Somewhere safe with somebody good.* New York, NY: G.P. Putnam's Sons.

Lewis, C. S. (1951). *Prince Caspian.* New York, NY: Macmillan.

Lewis, C. S. (1952). *The voyage of the Dawn Treader.* New York, NY: Macmillan.

Lively, P. (1994). *Oleander jacaranda: a childhood perceived: a memoir.* New York, NY: HarperCollins.

Mason, C. M. (1886/1989). *Home education.* Reprint, with foreword by John Thorley. Wheaton, IL: Tyndale House.

Mason, C. M. (1905/1989). *Ourselves.* Reprint, with foreword by by John Thorley. Wheaton, IL: Tyndale House.

Mason, C. M. (1925/1989). *A philosophy of education.* Reprint, with foreword by John Thorley. Wheaton, IL: Tyndale House.

Mason, C. M. (1904/1989). *School education.* Reprint, with foreword by John Thorley. Wheaton, IL: Tyndale House.

Pelling, C. B. R., & Plutarch. (2011). *Caesar.* Oxford: Oxford University Press.

Rien, P. (2016). *Love the house you're in: 40 ways to improve your home and change your life.* Boulder, CO: RB Boulder.

Bibliography

Seuss, Dr. (1957). *The cat in the hat.* New York, NY: Random House.

Shaffer, M. A., & Barrows, A. (2008). *The Guernsey Literary and Potato Peel Pie Society.* New York, NY: The Dial Press

Parents' Review Articles

All the articles cited below may be read on the AmblesideOnline website.

Ambler, [?] (1901). "Plutarch's Lives" as affording some education as a citizen. *Parents' Review, 7,* 521-527

Manders, E. K. (July 1967). We narrate and then we know. *Parents' Review, 2 (New Series),* 170-172

Parish, E.A. (1914). Imagination as a powerful factor in a well-balanced mind. *Parents' Review, 25,* 379-390.

Pennethorne, R. A. (1899). PNEU principles as illustrated by teaching. *Parents' Review, 10,* 549

Miscellaneous

Emerson, R. W. (1904). Written at Rome. *The complete works, Vol. IX, Poems.*

Emerson, R. W. (1904). Plutarch. *The complete works, Vol. X, Lectures and biographical sketches.*

Esolen, A. (2007, December 2). Top twenty books that nobody reads. *Touchstone Magazine-Mere Comments.* Retrieved from https://merecomments.typepad.com/merecomments/2007/12/top-twenty-book.html

Kern, A. (2013, October 21). Leisure, Plato's Republic, and American education. *Circe Institute.* Retrieved from https://www.circeinstitute.org/blog/leisure-plato%E2%80%99s-republic-and-american-education

The Practical Plutarch

Printed in Great Britain
by Amazon

25920561R00066